Rik Mayall is a writer/actor. His writing credits include: *The Young Ones* (with accompanying book); *Kick up the Eighties*; *Grim Tales*; and *The New Statesman*. As an actor he is well-known for his work in *The Comic Strip Presents*; *Filthy, Rich and Catflap*; *Blackadder*; as Rik in *The Young Ones*; as Alan B'Stard MP in *The New Statesman*; and for his role in the film *Drop Dead Fred*. He has also presented a trilogy of specially commissioned television films, *Mickey Love*, *Briefest Encounter* and *Dancing Queen*.

Adrian Edmondson is also a writer/actor. His writing credits include: *The Comic Strip Presents* and *The Dangerous Brothers*. In addition to his work as Vyvyan in *The Young Ones* he is also well-known for roles with the *Comic Strip*. He has had film roles in the Comic Strip feature film *Supergrass*, as well as *Honest, Decent and True*; *Filthy, Rich and Catflap*; *Newshounds*; and *If You See God, Tell Him*.

TOM

BOT

BOTTOM

THE SCRIPTS

RIK MAYALL & ADRIAN EDMONDSON

PENGUIN BOOKS
BBC BOOKS

THIS BOOK IS DEDICATED TO ED BYE

PENGUIN BOOKS
BBC BOOKS

Published by the Penguin Group and BBC Enterprises Ltd
Penguin Books Ltd, 27 Wrights Lane, London W8 5TZ, England
Penguin Books USA Inc., 375 Hudson Street, New York, New York 10014, USA
Penguin Books Australia Ltd, Ringwood, Victoria, Australia
Penguin Books Canada Ltd, 10 Alcorn Avenue, Toronto, Ontario, Canada M4V 3B2
Penguin Books (NZ) Ltd, 182–190 Wairau Road, Auckland 10, New Zealand

Penguin Books Ltd, Registered Offices: Harmondsworth, Middlesex, England

First published by BBC Books, a division of BBC Enterprises Ltd, 1992
Published in Penguin Books 1993
1 3 5 7 9 10 8 6 4 2

Printed in England by Clays Ltd, St Ives plc

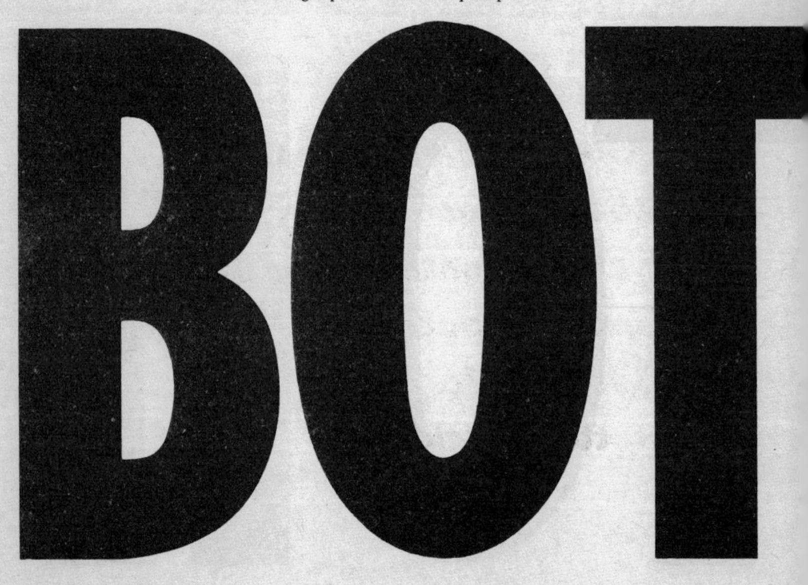

TOM

CONTENTS

BOTTOM SMELLS

SCENE ONE – FLAT

Richie and Eddie enter flat.

RICHIE Yes, what happened there? I just don't understand it, I made all the right moves, I winked, I smiled – one of my nice ones as well – I sat down very nicely, leant forward, put on my special eyes and said, 'Hello big tits, looking for some action tonight?' And what did she say?

EDDIE I think she said, 'No', didn't she?

RICHIE That's right! No! Blasted lesbians everywhere. They should have labels on them or something. I wasted half an hour on those two, prancing up and down, winking, clenching me buttocks. Backwards and forwards to the gents I was going. Look at this! Look at this!

He withdraws copious amounts of toilet paper from his flies.

RICHIE I've got armfuls of gonad enhancers down here!

EDDIE I don't think they were lesbians, Richie, cause they got off with those other blokes. Those handsomer, wittier, well, basically those two guys who didn't have a load of toilet paper stuffed down their trousers.

RICHIE Well you hardly helped did you? Stuffing a Vimto bottle down the front of your pants and shouting, 'Woo hoo! Looking for the Eiffel Tower girls?'

EDDIE I got a result.

RICHIE I don't call a kick in the knackers a result.

EDDIE A free drink.

RICHIE Oh yes, a kick in the knackers and a vodka and tonic in the face.

EDDIE Always keep your mouth open when you're insulting a lady.

RICHIE What a waste of time. Why won't they do it with me? Why? If only I could just get one of them to do it with me. Anybody. Just to do it with me. Just once. Just to find out what it's like. I mean just a snog'd do . . . no it wouldn't. I need to go the distance. I mean look, look all around you. It's Friday night and everywhere you look there's buildings full of people (*walks to window*) all doing it. All doing it and doing it and then stopping and having a fag and then doing it a bit more. There's not a single one of them saying, 'Hang on a minute. This really isn't fair. I mean, here's us doing it and doing it and doing it and there's poor old Richie, and he hasn't done it – *ever*. He hasn't got anyone to do it *to*. I'll tell you what, I'll pop down and do it to him for a bit and then pop back up. Would that be all right? I mean, it wouldn't hurt, would it? It'd be charitable. I mean, just think of all those acres and acres of ladies all lying there saying, 'Come on darling, let's do it' and the bloke's saying, 'No, I don't feel like doing it – the snooker's on.' Well I could be filling in for him! Providing a service. Could even charge. Might make a bit of money. Hey, Eddie, I've just thought of some . . . What on earth are you eating?

EDDIE Lard.

Pause.

RICHIE You are eating lard?

EDDIE Yes, well, I'm hungry and I'm too drunk to cook.

RICHIE All right Eddie. I can feel the elbow in me ribs. All right, I'll do one of my famous Friday night fry ups. Chuck us a couple of eggs.

The eggs go splat around Richie – on the cooker. The boys laugh together.

RICHIE Ha ha ha, the old ones are the best ones aren't they? Who needs girls when you've got your mates?! I tell you there's some things a girl just can't appreciate, and Richie's Friday night fry up is one of them. Oil!

Eddie is drinking the oil.

EDDIE Mazola.

He throws the bottle to Richie.

RICHIE Right then. A little dab of oil . . . my secret ingredient . . . . (*He tries to scrape a dried up concoction from the bottom of a pan.*) Come on out, you know you want to. Come on, you've only been in there a week.

Eddie is in the living room area and produces a pint of bitter from inside his coat. He falls onto the sofa.

Richie is still cooking.

RICHIE And then just the last couple of pints . . . .

Richie spots a couple opposite kissing.

RICHIE Oh!

He goes to the window and watches them through binoculars. They spot him.

RICHIE Lovely night.

He drops the binoculars and there is the sound of crashing and a dog barking below.

The couple gesture at him rudely and close the curtains.

Richie goes back inside.

RICHIE Why doesn't anyone ever want to have any sex with me?

EDDIE Well look on the bright side, Richie, at least you're not going to get any sexually transmitted diseases.

RICHIE You're right there. I'll be lucky to catch flu off a girl. In fact, the nearest I ever got to sex was when that bus conductress sneezed all over me this morning. Talk about the Green Line! (*Showing his scalp.*) Look there's still some of it in there. Oh Eddie, . . . I'm just so depressed.

EDDIE Oh cheer up, Richie, there's loads and loads of ugly birds in the world. One of 'em's bound to do it with you sooner or later. You just need to take a more scientific approach. Now, what have you got going for you? . . . Nothing. OK, so you're going to have to trick them into doing the nasty with you.

RICHIE What? You mean say, 'Ooooh, look over there at that big spider' and then quickly do it to her while she's not looking? I think that's called rape isn't it Eddie? Oh good plan, so I end up doing twenty years in prison getting loads of the wrong kind of sex, and you get to keep the flat. Very crafty. There must be *some* way I can get a woman to sleep with me. I mean she doesn't even have to *sleep* with me, it's the staying awake bit I'm interested in.

Eddie quaffs mightily and has an idea. Snaps his fingers.

EDDIE I think I've cracked it.

RICHIE Well you shouldn't have gone like that then. I'll get a splint.

EDDIE Why don't you pay me to come up with a good idea?

RICHIE All right then, you're on.

EDDIE How much?

RICHIE Your half of the taxi fare you owe me.

EDDIE What – so you give me one pound sixty and I fix you up with a fabulous orgy of slidy pump-pump?

RICHIE Yes.

EDDIE You're on. Right, give us the money.

RICHIE I've already given it to you.

EDDIE No you haven't.

RICHIE Yes I have. I'm letting you not give me one pound sixty, that's how I'm giving it to you.

EDDIE Don't start getting all clever just 'cos you know I'm drunk.

RICHIE I'm not, I'm not! Look, you owe me one pound sixty right?

EDDIE I do not! You owe me one pound sixty! And I'll thank you to hand it right over!!!

RICHIE All right, all right, don't get a bee in your bonnet, here you are. God, how did this happen?

EDDIE Thank you!!

Puts money in his pocket.

EDDIE Hey! I've just had a fantastic idea.

RICHIE Oh great!

Eddie drinks his pint.

RICHIE Well?

EDDIE What?

RICHIE What was the fantastic idea?

EDDIE To drink that!

RICHIE Oh!

EDDIE Only joking! Why not put an ad in a lonely hearts column?

RICHIE Yeah.

EDDIE Yeah, yeah. 'Ugly virgin desperately seeks sex of any description.'

RICHIE That is absolutely brilliant. Suave, sophisticated, witty . . . no come on, come on, let's be honest. Balding, sweaty, crusty . . . no hang on, we're going to have to be economical with the truth. Em, something buck . . . hot young buck . . . um, well nearing middle age, ageing buck, tepid ageing buck, no that's not quite right.

EDDIE What about badger?

RICHIE Tepid ageing badger?! No, no, I'm more a sort of a . . . .

EDDIE Hedgehog?

RICHIE No, fox, that's good. No that's good. No that *is* good. Tepid ageing fox. No, let's just forget the age and the heat.

EDDIE Stoat!!!

RICHIE Foxy stoat? Yeah, yeah, it's got a ring to it. Foxy stoat seeks . . . .

EDDIE Pig!!!

RICHIE Foxy stoat seeks pig? Shut up Eddie. This is very important. Let's see now. Foxy stoat on the prowl. Grrrrr, I like that. Musky, musky fox, musky sly old foxy stoat, minky musky sly old stoaty, stoaty stoat, oh this is ridiculous, I'm not getting anywhere. What do they normally put?

Eddie picks up the Hammersmith Bugle *and flicks to the back.*

EDDIE Hang on, here we are. Sad old gits section.

Taunting Richie.

Sad old *gits* section. Did you hear what I said?

RICHIE Yes.

EDDIE I said, 'Sad old git's section.'

RICHIE Please, I've only got so many ribs Noel Coward. What do they normally put?

EDDIE Well, he's not going to get very far is he? Gay!

RICHIE Don't knock it Eddie, cuts down the field for guys like us. Right let's have a look at this.

He grabs the paper.

RICHIE (*Reading.*) Gay gay gay gay gay gay – widow – gay. Ah widow! Busty raven-haired millionairess . . . gay. Gay, gay . . . hang on Eddie, this is the gay section.

EDDIE Yup!

RICHIE Oh look . . . Ooh, what's this – instant sex appeal!! You can get it in a bottle. Instant Sex Appeal.

EDDIE Let's have a look.

Staggers towards Richie and falls over the coffee table onto the floor.

RICHIE 'Fur-emonie' . . . no . . . 'Pheromone sex scent. Women cannot resist this powerful primitive love smell scientifically distilled from mystical African orchids.' Wow! Listen to this Eddie. 'One spray of Dr Glucklick's powerful female attractant and I was fighting women off in the disco.' Fighting them off! 'GS, Stalybridge.' Stalybridge! 'Thank you Dr Glucklick, your sex spray certainly changed my life. I now have ten girlfriends – every night!' This is sensational! Look, it's medically proven: 'This stuff attracts women like you would not believe – *Karachi Medical Gazette*. Available at all good sex shops.' This is it, Eddie, Girl City here we come. What do you think old chum?

Eddie throws up on him and the frying pan erupts into flames in the background.

RICHIE Nil desperandum!

SCENE TWO – SEX SHOP

Richie and Eddie open the door to the sex shop. Richie pushes Eddie in. There are a few dirty old men shambling round it grunting. Richie notices the grunting and motions to Eddie that they should do the same. Then . . .

RICHIE Are you sure this is the sex shop? Looks more like the plumber's.

They carry on looking round. The other men grunt a bit more and Eddie and Richie have to up the level of their grunting in response.

RICHIE Good grief! What on earth's that?

EDDIE Looks like a weapon of some sort . . . Hang on, it's got instructions on it . . . bloody Nora!

RICHIE I think this is the wrong section – I think this is car maintenance.

He holds up a couple of wrenches and other bits of ironmongery.

RICHIE That's an orange squeezer isn't it?

They gradually work their way to the counter.

MR SEX Can I help you sir?

EDDIE This is a sex shop isn't it?

MR SEX Yes.

Eddie bangs some money down on the counter.

EDDIE I'll have five quid's worth then. Ha ha ha.

MR SEX Very droll, sir. I've never heard that one before.

EDDIE Haven't you?! Shall I tell it again?

MR SEX No thank you, sir, I'd rather have a pineapple inserted violently into my rectum.

Slight pause.

EDDIE You've been working here too long, mate.

RICHIE (*Quietly.*) Get some pheromone.

MR SEX (*To Richie.*) Can I help you, sir?

RICHIE No.

MR SEX Do you wish to purchase anything to assist you with your sex life?

All the customers look at him.

RICHIE What are you implying? That I'm some sort of sexual inadequate? I have a very full and rich and varied sex life, thank you very much. I don't need anything from a shop like this.

MR SEX So you're not going to buy anything sir?

RICHIE Certainly not.

MR SEX Would you get out then sir?

Pause.

RICHIE No.

MR SEX Why not?

Pause.

RICHIE It's a secret.

(*Whispers to Eddie.*)

Get the pheromone, get the pheromone.

EDDIE OK. Two bottles of pheromone, please.

MR SEX Pardon?

EDDIE Two bottles of pheromone, please.

MR SEX (*Loudly.*) Pheromone. Oh yes. That's the sex spray for inadequate men who find it impossible to attract women?

Everyone looks at Eddie.

EDDIE That's the one, yes.

MR SEX (*To Richie.*) Isn't it, sir?

RICHIE I've got no idea. Not being a pervert I'm not up on these things.

MR SEX Your sex spray, gentlemen.

EDDIE I've got it!

RICHIE Fantastic! Give me mine! Let's go. I mean – well done, doctor.

EDDIE I'm not a doctor.

RICHIE Shut up. Now we can continue with our experiments. We are men of science.

EDDIE Are we?

RICHIE Yes, that's why we're so unfamiliar with your depraved little world. (*To Eddie.*) I got him there, Eddie – I'm winning this one.

MR SEX So you won't be needing the bumper stash of *Girlie World* that goes free with the pheromone this week?

RICHIE Absolutely not.

Privately despairs.

MR SEX Or these two free life-membership cards to Madame Fifi's sex palace.

Pause.

RICHIE Don't you dangle your filthy baubles in front of me you sex mad quisling. We live our lives on a higher plain than you do, buster, where truth and purity and virginity are the only things we respect.

EDDIE That's right. Let's get back to the flat, bung a bit of this on, get down the pub and see if we can pick up some birds.

RICHIE Yeah.

Panic. Pause. Richie and Mr Sex exchange glances.

Eddie and Richie run out.

SCENE THREE – BATHROOM

Eddie is staring at himself in the bathroom mirror.

EDDIE Hello baby, feeling mysteriously drawn to me are you? Well don't you worry, you can have me whenever you like. Form a queue girls, there's plenty for everybody.

Sticks out his tongue suggestively, then looks at it carefully in the mirror. He gets the razor and shaves his tongue.

Richie comes in.

RICHIE Blast these underpants! I've been soaking them for hours and I still can't get them off!

EDDIE What?

RICHIE You know I've only got one pair of pants?

EDDIE Yeah.

RICHIE Well the elastic went, so I had to glue them on.

EDDIE Have you tried Swarfega?

RICHIE Get out of it mate, this is Eternogum. Nothing'll shift this. I've been sitting in a bowl of petrol for the last two hours. I tell you, I'm a walking time bomb I am. One curry and I'll blow and I'll take half the street with me as well.

EDDIE Don't you worry Richie, within the hour some pheromone-crazed love goddess'll be ripping them off with her teeth.

RICHIE Do you really think so?

EDDIE No doubt about it.

RICHIE God I wonder what she'll find down there. I've had them on for three weeks. I'd better freshen them up a bit.

Goes to cabinet and starts pouring talcum powder and spraying deodorant down his pants.

A little bit of this. And a little bit of that.

He is contorting to dab himself all over.

And hey presto, who's got the loveliest tackle in Hammersmith? Oh yes, where's that biro?

Richie starts to biro in hairs on his chest.

Right. Chest hair. What do you think? Curly or straight? Curly's a bit suggestive, don't you think?

EDDIE Yeah, I'd go for curly.

RICHIE Yeah, curly it is.

EDDIE Not sure about the green, though.

RICHIE I know, but I used up all the black on my legs.

Richie spots something in the mirror.

RICHIE Oh oh, nose hair. Tweezers.

EDDIE What do you mean, tweezers? We don't have any tweezers.

RICHIE Well get some pliers then.

RICHIE Doesn't matter how much pheromone I put on. If some bird sees that coming at her out of the dark, she's likely to pull it and expect the butler to come in.

Eddie reappears with the pliers.

EDDIE Here we go. Which one is it?

RICHIE It's the third one on the left.

Eddie grips Richie's nose hair with the pliers.

EDDIE Brace yourself.

RICHIE Yes.

EDDIE 'Cos this might make your eyes water.

RICHIE OK.

He flings Richie about the room like a rag doll. It is extremely violent.

Richie punches Eddie in the knackers. Eddie falls over backwards and lands in the bath.

Richie looks in the mirror.

RICHIE Bastard!

Richie pulls the cabinet off the wall and smashes it over Eddie's head.

Eddie jumps out of the bath and lands a punch on Richie that makes him smash through the closed door.

Eddie tries to continue the fight.

RICHIE No Eddie, no. This is stupid.

EDDIE Yes.

RICHIE We're going out tonight to get some fantastic birds, remember. We don't have to take out our frustrations on each other, we can take them out on them. OK?

EDDIE OK.

RICHIE OK. Come on let's shake and make up.

They both shake their bodies independently and mime making up their faces.

BOTH Great gag.

EDDIE Yeah that's right, Richie, our crumpet free days are over. Listen to this . . . (*He reads from the bottle.*) 'Spray liberally . . . .

RICHIE Yeah.

EDDIE . . . go to a place with lots of females . . .

RICHIE Yeah.

EDDIE . . . and brace yourself.'

RICHIE How much do you think we should put on?

EDDIE Well, I've already put on half a bottle.

RICHIE What? Half a bottle? Are you insane? You'll be dead by morning. Death by sex – you'll just be lying there and they'll be doing it to you and doing it to you and doing it to you until . . . I think I'll put on half a bottle as well.

Starts to spray.

(*As he sprays himself.*) Little there, little bit here, little bit there . . . just in case . . . oooh! Right where's that packet of rubber johnnies we used to have?

EDDIE We stuck them on our heads remember? When Norman came round with that sherry?

RICHIE So we did. Great days. Ah well, not to worry. Let's get some more down the pub.

They exit.

SCENE FOUR – PUB

There is a commotion outside the entrance to the pub. Eddie and Richie are obviously having a lot of trouble with a pack of growling, yapping and barking dogs. They fight the dogs off and stumble into the pub, dishevelled and panting.

RICHIE Blimey when it said female, I didn't expect the term to be so broad. Right here we are. (*He sprays himself.*) Here we go. Death by sex, part one.

They gather themselves then have a good look round the pub. There are a couple of girls, Kate and Jenny, sitting at a table, a few scattered old men and a couple of normal women at the bar next to a couple of men.

EDDIE Look at that crackling bit of crumpet.

We see a woman at the bar.

RICHIE Right, that one's got my number on it. I'll see you later old pal – I'm going in.

EDDIE OK. Good luck, skipper.

Richie approaches the woman, wafting as he goes.

RICHIE (*In a spooky voice.*) Yes. Give in . . . give in to your cravings . . . .

WOMAN I beg your pardon?

He is making motions like a hypnotiser, trying to lure her away from the bar.

RICHIE Do as you are bid . . . you cannot help yourself . . . come back to my place because we're going to have it off.

He backs into a very large man returning from the toilets.

MAN What do you think you're doing with my wife?

EDDIE He's going to have it off with her.

The man grabs Richie by the bollocks.

MAN I don't think he is.

He gives Richie's bollocks a good wrench.

MAN I don't think he's capable any more.

WOMAN No . . . darling don't hurt them, I think it's shocking they send them back into the community so soon . . . .

RICHIE Yes, that's right, we're mere loonies – we mean no harm.

The man lets him go. Eddie and Richie make loony noises and move away.

RICHIE (*In loony voice.*) Come back to my place, we're going to have it off . . . I'm mad! (*To Eddie*) You see it worked.

EDDIE Did it?

RICHIE Course it did. If it hadn't been for that gorilla, I would have been well away. Did you see her? She was mesmerised! And I'll tell you what . . . .

EDDIE What?

RICHIE It's loosened up my pants a bit too.

EDDIE This is your lucky day.

RICHIE You're not wrong there. Come on, we'll get the drinks in and then we'll prowl. Landlord, two halves of mild please.

EDDIE In pint glasses!

LANDLORD Certainly Eddie, and how are we tonight?

EDDIE Yup.

LANDLORD (*Sniffs.*) Phwaw, smells like the drains have gone again.

He goes off to get the drinks. Eddie and Richie look round for their next candidates. They spy Kate and Jenny.

EDDIE Cor, look at those couple of stunners down there.

RICHIE Wow! Do you think they're Starbirds.

EDDIE Yeah bound to be mate. Either that or topless models.

RICHIE Look at the way they're sitting, they're screaming for it.

EDDIE Do you think it'll work?

RICHIE Bound to mate. Two girls all alone in a pub. Why do you think they're here? They want to have it off with someone. Come on.

LANDLORD That'll be one pound sixty please, gents.

EDDIE Yeah. Cheers! Just put it on the slate, Dick.

LANDLORD You haven't got a slate.

EDDIE Yes we have.

LANDLORD No you haven't.

EDDIE I demand to see the landlord.

LANDLORD I am the landlord.

EDDIE I know.

LANDLORD We have this conversation every night. One pound sixty.

Richie gives him the money begrudgingly.

RICHIE All right, here you are. Vampire.

EDDIE Leech.

RICHIE Bloodsucker.

EDDIE Parasite.

RICHIE Usurer.

LANDLORD Shut up.

EDDIE (*To Richie.*) It's always worth a try.

RICHIE Absolutely. Speaking of which – 'let the tournament commence.'

They move to the girls' table and start wafting. No effect. Then Richie prods Kate.

RICHIE Excuse me, excuse me.

Kate looks at him questioningly. He smiles sexily. She doesn't understand and goes back to talking with her friend. Richie continues to waft.

KATE Is there something wrong?

RICHIE No, there's everything right, my love.

EDDIE (*Pointing at Jenny.*) Is that one mine?

RICHIE Yes, that's your bird.

EDDIE Right, I'd better get started then. Right, so what is it to be then? Mild or bitter?

RICHIE Or straight back to our place?

KATE I'm sorry, look we really don't want a drink.

RICHIE I think you do.

Richie sprays under his armpit and sticks it over Kate's face.

RICHIE Are you sure?

KATE All right, if you must, I'll have a Coke.

RICHIE Bingo! It bloody works. Eddie you get the drinks in. I'll keep the birds white hot.

Eddie goes to the bar.

RICHIE So . . . little baby . . . what might your little name be today?

KATE My little name's Kate today, same as it was yesterday.

RICHIE Ha ha ha. (*Laughs off the sarcasm.*) I say, what a lovely blouse, it's very special isn't it? Do you often wear blouses? Or sometimes do you wear a jumper? I suppose it depends on the weather really doesn't it? I sometimes wear a jumper, there again sometimes I wear a cardy . . . Tell me, do you like to take people's underpants off with your teeth?

Kate reacts. We hear a commotion at the bar.

LANDLORD You haven't got a slate!

EDDIE Extortioner!

RICHIE Parasite!

LANDLORD Shut up!

Eddie comes back with the coke.

EDDIE Here we go.

RICHIE . . . I suppose if you're wearing dentures . . . .

EDDIE (*Holding the coke bottle.*) Hey here's a good one – anyone fancy a quick gander at the Eiffel Tower?

RICHIE Yes, this is frightfully good . . . No it's not. Eddie, no, no! Don't do that because . . .

Richie stands up.

. . . I think it's time to go to the toilet . . . Eddie . . . wouldn't you like to come to the toilet with me?

EDDIE No, I wouldn't.

He mimes condoms behind the heads of Kate and Jenny.

EDDIE I get it – johnnies! I've just remembered girls – I'm desperate to go, keep yourselves hot, we shall be but a moment. Adieu, adieu, to yer, and yer and yer.

RICHIE Edward Hitler! Will you get into the lavatory with me this instant.

He realises everyone is looking at him.

We're toilet inspectors.

They go into the toilets.

SCENE FIVE – PUB TOILETS

EDDIE The coast is clear.

RICHIE Right, let's go. Nadgers, what kind do you want?

EDDIE Rubber ones!

RICHIE Yeah but there's ribbed, there's ticklers and there's ultra-sensitive.

EDDIE Ripped!?

RICHIE Yeah.

EDDIE Who's gonna want a ripped condom?

RICHIE That must be for people who want to get pregnant. Well, I don't think ultra-sensitive's our style, do you? Right then, tickler it is . . . Ooh nadgers! What colour?

EDDIE What have they got?

RICHIE There's black, there's gold, there's Union Jack or there's leopard skin.

EDDIE Which do you think is the most romantic?

RICHIE Union Jack of course.

EDDIE Well, Union Jack tickler then.

RICHIE Okey dokey. Ooh nadgers. What flavour?

EDDIE Flavour?!!

RICHIE Yeah. There's banana, strawberry, peanut butter, marmite or cheese and onion?

EDDIE Well everyone likes cheese and onion don't they?

RICHIE Of course they do. Okey dokey then, cheese and onion flavour Union Jack tickler it is. Bagsy me go first with it.

EDDIE No, no. Get two.

RICHIE Get two?

EDDIE Yeah.

RICHIE Wildman.

He puts 50p in the machine and pulls the handle. Nothing happens.

Bastard! . . . Bastard! Give me my rubber johnnies.

He hits the machine a few times.

EDDIE Hang on, hang on, hang on, hang on, hang on. I'm the DIY expert. Right, let's have a look at the little fella. Yeah, I think I see the problem.

RICHIE What is it?

Eddie whacks the machine with his fist. Nothing happens. Meanwhile the husband enters unseen and has a pee while watching what's going on.

RICHIE Give me my johnnies, give me my johnnies. There's two birds out there in the bar who are just screaming for it. Give me my johnnies.

Eddie has clocked the husband and taps Richie on the shoulder.

RICHIE Get off Eddie. Give me my johnnies. I just want to do it and do it and do it to those two birds at the ba . . . aagh!

Richie sees the husband.

HUSBAND You want to what?

EDDIE He wants to do it and do it and do it to those two birds at the bar.

The husband comes up to face Richie. Slight pause, then he hits Richie in the face and walks out. Richie's head careers into the johnnie machine which disgorges johnnies like a one-armed bandit onto Richie's head.

RICHIE Eddie look! More johnnies than it's humanly possible to use in a week!

EDDIE Right!

Eddie starts to spray the pheromone into his mouth and is visibly suffering from an overdose.

RICHIE (*With handfuls of condoms.*) Come on! That should do for a week. Let's get out there before our two crumpets go off the boil.

SCENE SIX – PUB

Richie and Eddie emerge from the toilet. The table where the girls were is empty.

RICHIE Oh no! Someone's nicked our birds.

EDDIE Come on Richie, let me at 'em. I'm a sex typhoon. Hello baby . . .

RICHIE Eddie, Eddie, calm down that's a chair.

EDDIE Yeah. It's a bit of all right isn't it?

RICHIE Eddie, calm down. Someone's nicked our crumpets. Oh no – there they are . . . .

They cross to the table where Kate and Jenny are sitting. As they pass the bar, Eddie makes an amorous move towards the husband.

RICHIE Eddie no – wrong one.

Richie puts on his loony act for the husband's benefit and they continue to Kate and Jenny's table.

RICHIE Ha ha ha ha ha. Oh so you've moved tables. Of course, how silly of me, it's much more romantic in a booth isn't it birds?

KATE Look, I'm sorry but we're having a private conversation.

RICHIE That's all right. You just carry on. We'll sit here and listen.

Richie and Eddie sit.

RICHIE But you'd better hurry up, we haven't got all night.

JENNY No, I'm sorry, we'd really rather be on our own.

RICHIE Oh. Oh ha ha ha ha ha ha. Trying to decide which one of us you want to have are you? Well before you decide, let me tell you that 'tiny' Eddie and I share the same flat, so don't worry, you'll both be waking up in the same house.

EDDIE Have me, have me, I'm a love albatross.

Falls down.

Girls react.

RICHIE Ha ha ha. Although if you play your cards right you could both wind up sleeping in the same bed.

He flashes what he thinks are meaningfully sexy eyes.

KATE I'm sorry, you've got the wrong idea. We're really not interested, besides which we're lesbians.

RICHIE Well you'll be used to it then . . . YOU'RE WHAT?!!!

KATE We're les . . .

RICHIE Yes, I heard what you said. Is this some kind of joke? Because if it is I don't think it's very funny.

JENNY Come on Kate, let's go.

RICHIE Wait a minute. You sit down there young lady, I bought you a Coca Cola in good faith. That's eighty pence you've hoodwinked out of me – eighty pence! When I said, 'Hello my darling would you like a Coca Cola?' did you say, 'No, thank you, I'm terribly sorry, I'm a lesbian'? No you didn't, not a bit of it, you said, 'Thank you very much, that'll be lovely.'

KATE No I didn't, I said, 'Oh all right, if you must.'

RICHIE Oh all right, there's no need to be so pedantic. The fact is you owe me eighty pence.

KATE What do you mean?

RICHIE Well you're not going to sleep with me are you?

KATE Here's your eighty pence. Come on, let's go.

RICHIE (*Suddenly hurt.*) You're going? No wait, wait, look . . .

The girls head for the door, Richie runs after them.

. . . this is silly. This is so silly. Look, look, look I'm terribly sorr . . . Look, what the hell, let's waive the eighty pence – you know it's Saturday night. Who cares? Look, look, OK I'm sorry. I have been terribly intolerant, it's not your fault that you're lesbians . . . look, please give me one more chance, come back to my place and I'll cure you.

The girls walk out.

What did I say?

They have left. Richie has to raise his voice even more.

RICHIE No, no. Don't go. Please. I've got the same ideas about women as you have. I've got loads of magazines at home, you can come back with me and we'll all read them together. I've got every mail order catalogue since 1983 and they just flop open at the lingerie pages. No! Wait, wait. I even taped the *Clothes Show* special on beachwear – we could take all our clothes off and watch them in our pants!

Pauses and turns. It turns into embarrassement as he realises the whole pub was listening.

RICHIE Yes, is there something wrong?

They lose interest.

Huh! Saturday night. Oh well, may as well have another drink. Landlord, I shall have a large . . . .

LANDLORD Time gentlemen, please.

RICHIE You are a c . . . .

LANDLORD Out!

Richie hears a voice behind him.

EDDIE Hi baby. Oh you smell great – let's do it.

RICHIE Eddie, get a grip.

EDDIE Lovely aren't you, lovely, lovely, lovely.

RICHIE Eddie, no.

EDDIE Richie, yes.

RICHIE Right, I'm off.

Richie exits and is immediately attacked by dogs. He dashes back into the pub.

EDDIE Changed your mind have you, dearie? Well come on then, plant a big one right on me kisser.

Richie punches Eddie.

Fin.

BOTTOM GAS

SCENE ONE – THE FLAT – LIVING-ROOM/KITCHEN

The gas fire is blazing away. In the kitchen all the gas burners are alight. The oven is on with the door open. Richie and Eddie are huddled round the table playing poker. They are both trying to put on poker faces as they gamble. There is a pile of bits of paper in the middle of the table.

RICHIE Right, I'll bet another week's worth of washing up.

He puts in a piece of paper which says 'washing up' on it.

EDDIE I'll see your week's washing up, and I'll raise you four trips to the laundrette, 3p in *real* money and one cleaning and disinfecting, right round the back, of the lavatory bowl.

RICHIE Well that's cleaned me out.

He pushes all his 'chips' forward.

EDDIE Right, what have you got?

RICHIE Three pairs.

EDDIE What do you mean three pairs? You're only allowed five cards.

RICHIE Oh! Shit! (*Hiding a card under his cushion.*) Sorry, two pairs. Well, two and a half pairs.

EDDIE Stand up.

RICHIE No.

EDDIE Come on.

RICHIE I can't, I've got a hernia.

EDDIE No you haven't.

RICHIE I have, all the excitement's just given me a hernia.

EDDIE Look, stand up or I *will* give you a hernia.

RICHIE All right, all right.

EDDIE Cards!

Richie gets up to reveal a lot of cards on his chair.

EDDIE Thank you. Shoes!

RICHIE Oh, don't be ridiculous, I haven't got any in my shoes.

EDDIE Yes you have – I saw you fold them up and put them in there.

Richie takes off his shoes and empties them of cards.

EDDIE Underpants.

RICHIE Oh Eddie, those are my best ones.

EDDIE Look, I'm not angry. It's just that we're playing with a deck of twelve cards here.

RICHIE Oh, all right.

Eddie stacks them all back into the pack.

EDDIE Right, let's get on with the game.

RICHIE Right. What have you got?

EDDIE Five kings.

RICHIE Damn, you get me every time.

EDDIE (*Laughing.*) Ha ha ha. Come here me lovelies. (*Raking in all the slips of paper.*) Let's see what we've got then . . . one cleaning of the toilet, two cleanings of the bath, two months' tea in bed, thirteen trips to the laundrette, seventeen pence, a book of 'Victorian' postcards, a signed photo of Sue Carpenter, and no more washing up until 1993.

Richie reacts.

Ooh, and a Chinese burn. I think I'll have that now. (*Rolls up Richie's sleeve.*)

RICHIE One of these days I'm going to learn the rules of that game mate, then you'll really be for it. Oww!

There is a ringing at the door.

RICHIE Well, who on earth could that be at this time of the day?

EDDIE Well I'm not expecting anyone.

RICHIE Nor am I.

EDDIE Well it must be for someone else then.

RICHIE Yeah.

EDDIE Right. Another game?

RICHIE You bet!

Ring!

EDDIE Seven card stud or crazy eights?

RICHIE Makes no difference to me, mate. I don't know the rules.

EDDIE Right, one card slam it is then.

RICHIE Okey dokey.

Eddie slams card down.

EDDIE Oh! Twelve quid!

RICHIE Bloody hell! (*Pays up.*) No wonder they always shoot each other on those river boats.

Doorbell rings again.

Oh God, it's him, he's breaking my concentration. Answer the door, Eddie, this man's costing me a fortune.

EDDIE I don't have to mate – not for the next six years. (*Produces paper.*)

Doorbell.

RICHIE All right, I'm coming.

Doorbell.

All right, all right, who do you think I am? Speedy Gonzales?

Ring!

Richie opens the door. Hits the man's finger which is just moving towards the bell press again.

RICHIE Right! That's enough of that. That's my electricity you're using you know. I'm not the Aga Khan.

Richie sees the man is wearing the uniform of the Gas Board.

Cripes! It's the Gas Man.

GAS MAN Hello, I wonder if I could just read your meter?

Richie lookes round trying to find Eddie with fear in his face, then turns and shouts at the top of his voice right into the Gas Man's face.

RICHIE Hello Mr Gas Man!!!!!!

GAS MAN Er, yes, hello.

EDDIE You what?

RICHIE HELLO MR GAS MAN!!!

GAS MAN Yes, hello again, I wonder if I could just read your . . .

EDDIE Mr who?

RICHIE GAS MAN!!! GAS MAN!!! GAS MAN!!!

Eddie finally gets it and rushes round the flat turning off all the gas appliances.

Richie looks panicked.

GAS MAN (*Slowly, as if to a loony.*) Do you have someone who looks after you? Could I see them, because I need to read your meter.

Eddie appears, panting.

EDDIE Who is it, darling?

RICHIE It's the gas man.

GAS MAN Yes, I think we've established that.

EDDIE Well don't leave him out there in the cold, dreamboat – show him in.

They all come into the living room.

GAS MAN Oh, it's nice and warm in here. Right, I'll just have a look at your meter if I may. Oh yes, here's the little fella.

EDDIE Oh you don't want to look at that, mate. It's very boring. I had a look at it once – fell into a coma.

Gas man laughs condescendingly.

GAS MAN Actually, that's where you're wrong, 'cos the ones in this street are particularly interesting.

RICHIE (*Nearly sick with worry.*) Oh really? Why's that then?

GAS MAN Well, there's been a complaint from someone in this street that they're paying too much for their gas. We've got to check all the meters in the street and make sure everything's OK.

RICHIE (*Feigning mild interest, but hiding terror.*) Oh. Have you checked next door yet?

GAS MAN No, they're next.

RICHIE (*The same if only more worried.*) Oh!

GAS MAN That is if I don't knock off before I get to them.

Eddie slips out.

GAS MAN And it's quarter to six now.

Eddie comes back with cricket bat.

So if it takes me fifteen minutes to do this one, I probably won't get to him till tomorrow morning. That's odd.

Gas man stands. Eddie hides the cricket bat.

RICHIE What, is there some sort of problem . . . officer?

GAS MAN No – it's just a strange reading.

RICHIE Really? What does it say?

GAS MAN Nought, nought, nought, nought, nought, nought, nought.

RICHIE That'd be right. We don't use gas. Do we Eddie?

EDDIE I don't even know what it is mate. What is gas?

RICHIE All right, all right, don't spoil it.

GAS MAN How do you keep it so warm in here then?

RICHIE (*Thinks.*) We make love.

Gas Man looks shocked.

RICHIE No, not together, you understand. On our own . . . if you know what I mean . . . lots.

Richie shrugs in desperation.

GAS MAN That's very interesting. It takes all sorts don't it? Right, I think I'll be on my way then.

Richie runs round dramatically and blocks the door.

RICHIE No. No.

EDDIE Wait!

GAS MAN What?

EDDIE Do you want a cup of tea?

GAS MAN Tea? No, I don't think I will, thank you very much.

RICHIE You must! You must! You must drink our tea! It's the best tea in London! Sit down and drink it for about twelve minutes.

GAS MAN (*Trying to placate a madman.*) Right, yes, I'd love a cup of tea. Thank you very much.

Pause.

EDDIE Right, I'll put the kettle on then.

He strides up and is about to use the gas stove to heat the water.

GAS MAN Er, put the kettle on?

EDDIE . . . Yes. Er. Put the kettle on . . . the floor, because we won't be needing that because we don't use gas. Er . . . how do we usually make the tea?

RICHIE We usually use the water from the hot tap, don't we?

EDDIE Yes, that's what we do. (*To gas man.*) Funny the things you forget, eh?

Richie laughs. Gas Man flinches.

RICHIE Nice trousers.

Pause.

They . . . they remind me of a story I know – a long story – lasts about fifteen minutes. Once upon a time there was a big forest and in the middle of the forest there lived some trousers, called Dave . . . . Well come on Eddie, we're dying for some lovely cups of refreshing tea.

GAS MAN Isn't your water heated by a gas boiler then?

EDDIE Yes. Er, no it isn't because we don't use gas. Er, because we don't know what it is.

GAS MAN Then why are you using the hot tap then?

RICHIE We get the cold water from the hot tap – that way we save wear and tear on the cold tap.

GAS MAN How do you heat the water for the tea then?

RICHIE We don't, we have it cold. Don't we Eddie?

EDDIE Yes, that's right. We have it . . . cold?

Gas Man looks at the boiler on the kitchen wall.

GAS MAN But your pilot light seems to be on.

RICHIE Is it? (*Looks.*) Oh my God, it's caught fire.

Opens the panel and blows out the pilot light.

That was a close one, wasn't it?

EDDIE Here we go then. Three mugs of steaming cold tea. Better drink it before it gets warm.

RICHIE Well. Cheerio then! This is the best tea in London. Mmmmmmm!

Richie takes a cup and has to drink it and enjoy it. He gets tea leaves round his mouth.

Mmmm, lovely. Well come on Eddie, you're not drinking yours.

EDDIE Yes, I know – I'm watching you enjoying yours.

RICHIE Well come on, do your fair share you bastard! (*Then to gas man.*) And you!

GAS MAN Erm . . . No, I don't think I'll bother if you don't mind.

RICHIE Bloody hell, I drank mine! Look it's not fair!

GAS MAN No, I think I'll be on my way.

RICHIE No you won't. You'll sit down there and drink your tea. Come on, all of it . . . now!

Gas Man drinks.

GAS MAN Thank you very much. Lovely! Right. I'll just be on my way then.

He gets up to leave.

RICHIE No! You can't go.

GAS MAN Why not?

RICHIE (*Thinking fast.*) Because I love you!

GAS MAN What?

RICHIE I love you, and I can't live without you, at least not for the next eight minutes.

GAS MAN Right that's it, I'm off.

RICHIE You stay where you are, mate.

GAS MAN No, I'm afraid I'm on my way now. Now come on . . . .

He gets up and starts for the door.

RICHIE You're not going anywhere.

Richie punches the Gas Man, who falls to the floor banging his head. Eddie hits him on the head with a frying pan. Richie punches him repeatedly.

RICHIE You're not going anywhere, mate. Mate? Mate?

Pause.

Eddie and Richie look at each other.

RICHIE Eddie, you've killed him!

EDDIE (*Dropping frying pan.*) I never touched him.

RICHIE Yeah, but the frying pan did, didn't it? – And you were touching that at the time.

EDDIE Bollocks, you killed him. He was dead before he hit the ground.

RICHIE Well then why did you hit him with the frying pan?

EDDIE For fun.

Pause. They look at the body. It sinks in.

RICHIE Oh God . . . what are we going to do?

EDDIE About twenty five years I think.

RICHIE No, rubbish, it was an accident. He fell over on his way to the door . . . .

EDDIE That's right. And banged himself repeatedly over the head with a frying pan.

RICHIE You're right, we're done for. (*To body.*) Wake up, you bastard. (*He hits the body again.*) You bastard.

Eddie hits Richie with frying pan.

EDDIE Calm down.

RICHIE I am calm. Aaaggggh!! (*To body.*) You bastard! You bastard! Aagh! Aagh!

Eddie hits Richie with the frying pan again.

EDDIE Calm down you hysterical girl's blouse.

RICHIE I'm sorry, I'm sorry. OK. (*Takes deep breaths.*) Oh God, oh God, this is real.

EDDIE That's right, so we've got to be sensible.

RICHIE Sensible. Let's eat him. No, sorry, stupid idea, we're not allowed to use the gas, are we?

EDDIE Now, what do they do in the movies?

RICHIE They buy a ticket, sit in the dark and watch the film. Now stick to the point for Christ's sake.

EDDIE No, I mean in the films themselves. I mean, what did Michael Caine do in *Jack the Ripper*?

RICHIE He was the one that caught him wasn't he?

EDDIE No, no, no, no, no, that was his friend, what's his name, Mason, James Mason.

RICHIE No! He was the Ripper.

EDDIE No he wasn't!

RICHIE He was so!

EDDIE He was not, they never caught the Ripper.

RICHIE Didn't they? Well how'd he get away with it then? Because that's what we need to do. Now.

EDDIE Well . . . he . . . er . . . ran off into the night, laughing like a maniac, with his cape flapping behind him.

RICHIE Did he? Well let's do that then! Come on, let's get out of here.

EDDIE Hang on Richie. What about the body?

RICHIE What about the body?

EDDIE Well we can't just leave it here.

RICHIE Why not? It's dead, it's not going anywhere.

EDDIE Exactly my point, Moriarty. Leaving a dead body in our own flat would point the finger somewhat don't you think?

RICHIE OK, well, we'll cut it up. And scatter it round Old London Town. Where's the scissors?

EDDIE Yeah yeah. (*Thinks.*) No. Richie, we can't prance around the whole of London in your Batman cape throwing bits of dead body everywhere. Someone'll see us.

RICHIE Nobody'll see because of all the pea soup floating about the place.

EDDIE Richie, walking around London, flinging bits of dead body around is a non-starter. Hey, mabye he's not dead, maybe he's just stunned. Why don't you give him the kiss of life?

RICHIE Yeah! No, I will not you sad pervy. We've got a dead body in the house and your first idea is to sexually assault it.

EDDIE Oh, come on, you've always wanted to find out what snogging's really like.

Richie thinks about it.

RICHIE Oh, all right.

He kneels down.

EDDIE Look, just hold his nose, yank his mouth open and blow a load of air into his lungs.

RICHIE Well that doesn't sound very romantic, Eddie. Good grief, it's no wonder you're still single.

EDDIE Get out the way, I'll do it.

RICHIE Get off. Get off. He's my bird. Do you want a fight about it?

EDDIE Well get on with it then.

RICHIE All right, I am.

Richie quivers with excitement as he makes to kiss him then blows feebly from a distance.

EDDIE Oh, get out the way. I'll give him a go with this.

Brandishes bicycle pump.

EDDIE Hold the end in his mouth.

Richie does so. Eddie pumps furiously.

EDDIE How's he looking?

RICHIE Fatter! Mind you, the colour's come back to his cheeks.

EDDIE Yeah. But it shouldn't be bright purple. Oh this isn't going to work.

Pulls out pump. Farty noise.

RICHIE Is he related to you?

EDDIE Hang on. I've had a better idea.

Eddie puts on rubber gloves.

RICHIE No, no Eddie, no. Have you no shame? No, it's not natural. Besides which, I've got to do the washing up in those later.

Eddie wrenches the wires from the wall amid sparks and smoke.

RICHIE Oh! That's what you're doing! I thought it was . . . .

EDDIE Right, open his shirt

Richie kneels in a nursy way.

RICHIE Right! Now, I'm just going to undo your zip. It's nothing sexy, it's actually quite good for you. So you lie back and relax – that's what you're doing anyway isn't it?

EDDIE Oh get out the way. I'll do it. Here, hold these.

Hands Richie the wires. Richie fries. Lights dim up and down. Eddie opens the gas man's shirt.

EDDIE Right, give me the electrodes back. Stop dancing, he's not impressed you know. Stop messing about.

Grabs the electrodes.

RICHIE Oooooh!

EDDIE Right, here goes.

Tries the electrodes on his chest, then on his temples, then up his nose.

EDDIE No, it's no good – he's dead all right.

Pulls wires out.

Well, how are we going to get rid of the body?

RICHIE Well, I'm still all in favour of eating him. It doesn't matter about the gas problem, we could have him cold.

EDDIE I don't like the look of him.

RICHIE Well, that's not a problem, we'll sellotape a picture of Sue Carpenter over his face – you'd soon tuck in then wouldn't you? I know I would.

EDDIE (*Handing him a knife and fork.*) All right, here you go then.

RICHIE Oh great. Here we go. Oh God, there's so much to choose from isn't there? Tum-ti-tum-ti-tum.

Richie stabs the fork into his goolies.

RICHIE Hey wait a minute. I've got a better idea. We don't have to eat him. We'll get someone else to eat him for us.

Picks up telephone. Glances outside.

Great, he's still open.
Hello Amal, how's the kebab business? Yeah. Yeah. Yeah all right, I don't want a conversation about it – it was just a conversational pleasantry. Well, how are you off for meat? Yeah? Well bugger you then.

Slams phone down.

Damn! No good. He said his alsatian got run over this morning so he's all right for meat for the rest of the week. What are we going to do with the body?

EDDIE What body?

The body is nowhere to be seen.

RICHIE Eddie, that is absolutely . . .

Richie crashes to the floor.

RICHIE . . . pathetic.

The body is under the carpet.

EDDIE Yeah, well it's early days. We've got to flatten it out a bit.

RICHIE Oh right.

They jump on the body.

RICHIE That's not bad, actually. That's pretty good. You know, I think we're going to get away with this.

EDDIE All right, I'll pretend to be a policeman.

RICHIE Okey doke.

Goes out. Comes back.

EDDIE Hello, hello, hello. What's that dead body doing under the carpet?

RICHIE Damn!

EDDIE Hey, I've just had an idea – why don't we stick him on a bus?

RICHIE Yeah! No, it's no good. The conductor'd notice when he didn't pay his fare.

EDDIE No, no, why don't we stick him *on* a bus.

RICHIE (*Yells.*) Because the conductor'd notice when he didn't pay his fare!!

EDDIE I mean on the roof!

RICHIE (*Yelling.*) You don't get conductors on the roof!!!

EDDIE Exactly. That's what makes the plan so flawless! Look – we grab him, and when the next bus comes along we just chuck him onto the roof. Off goes the body. Who knows where. Nobody'll find him till he gets to the depot and even then they won't know where he's come from.

RICHIE Yeah. Well not unless they look at his pocket book and see that the last job he had today was here. Ah . . . er . . .

EDDIE Well that's no problem.

Goes into the Gas Man's bag.

Ah look! He's got a fiver in here. That'll come in handy . . .

Sits at table.

Right then, where are we? Ah, here we are.

Licks pencil thoughtfully. Then writes.

'No problem with the meter in this flat, don't check for another three hundred years. Nice people, especially the bloke with the glasses, who *wasn't* holding a frying pan. Nice atmos altogether really.'

RICHIE All right Dickens, get on with it.

EDDIE 'Left in high spirits to indulge in my hobby of bus surfing.' Great. That should do it. Right come on Richie, let's grab hold of the stiff, avoid the obvious joke, and chuck him onto the next number nine.

RICHIE Oh, quick, Eddie, there's one at the lights!

They haul the body to the window and start swinging it.

EDDIE One, two, three . . . .

GAS MAN (*Groans.*) Urgggh.

They look at each other.

GAS MAN Bloody hell, my head.

BOTH Agggggggghhhhh!!!!

GAS MAN Ow! Urgh! Where am I? What happened?

RICHIE You banged your head on the frying pan Eddie was holding.

EDDIE Several times.

RICHIE And then you tried to throw yourself out of the window.

GAS MAN Oh God it's the loony – let me out of here.

RICHIE Yes, you've got no time to go next door now. You'd better knock off straight away. You'd better get home to your wife.

GAS MAN Right, yes . . . I haven't got a wife.

EDDIE That'll be the amnesia mate.

Gas Man exits.

GAS MAN Yes! I wonder where I live?

Falls downstairs. Richie slams the door shut.

RICHIE You stupid stupid bastard! I knew you'd get us into trouble.

EDDIE He looked all right to me.

RICHIE I'm not talking about him. I'm talking about nicking next door's gas supply. What time is it now?

EDDIE Quarter past six.

RICHIE Is it? Right, that means we've got until nine o'clock tomorrow, which is . . . .

They look at their watches and try to compute.

EDDIE Ooh, that's a difficult one . . . there's a five in it . . . No . . . four hours, twenty-seven minutes.

RICHIE Is it? Ooh yes, that's right – I was just about to say that. That means we've got four hours and twenty-seven minutes to get in next door and remove that illegal gas pipeline we connected to next door's mains, right? I'll keep him talking and you go into the kitchen and do all the dangerous stuff, OK?

EDDIE That sounds just a trifle unfair to me.

RICHIE Oh, that's the spirit. Have you got the wrench?

EDDIE No, it's just my underpants are a bit tight.

RICHIE Ha ha.

He bops Eddie. Eddie bops him back. They bop each other again. Richie tries to stop it.

No Eddie, no. This is no time for merriment. We've got to go in and do a job matey. OK?

EDDIE OK.

RICHIE Right. Let's hasten to the neighbour's. Shouldn't be any problem – he's a nice enough man.

EDDIE Now that's true.

SCENE TWO – OUTSIDE NEIGHBOUR'S DOOR

They ring the neighbour's doorbell and he answers.

RICHIE Evening Mr Rottweiler.

ROTTWEILER What is it?

RICHIE Just a friendly visit. May we come in?

ROTTWEILER Bugger off. I've got a bird upstairs.

RICHIE But we've brought round half a bottle of sherry.

ROTTWEILER Ta very much. (*Takes the bottle.*) Anything else?

LOLLY (*Voice inside.*) Who is it darling?

ROTTWEILER It's them bastards from next door, I won't be a tick.

EDDIE Have you got a real woman in there?

RICHIE Can we have a look?

ROTTWEILER Sod off!

RICHIE No, go on, go on, just a peek.

EDDIE D'you mind if I get my camera?

ROTTWEILER (*Grabbing them.*) Look, don't make me angry. Something very special's happened to me – I'm in love. It's the real thing. So I don't want you two jerks coming round messing things up. D'you understand? If I see either of you again tonight – I'll kill you.

Slams the door. Richie immediately rings on bell. He opens it again.

ROTTWEILER What?!

RICHIE My fingers are stuck in the door.

Rottweiler slams the door. This time, Richie's willy gets stuck in the door.

SCENE THREE – EXTERIOR KITCHEN/ROTTWEILER'S BEDROOM

Eddie is crawling along the drainpipe towards Rottweiler's flat.

RICHIE Keep your head down.

EDDIE What?

RICHIE Keep your head down.

EDDIE Pardon?

RICHIE It doesn't matter.

Eddie crawls back to Richie.

EDDIE What?

RICHIE It doesn't matter.

EDDIE What doesn't matter?

RICHIE What I just said.

EDDIE What did you just say?

RICHIE It doesn't matter.

EDDIE No, no I heard that. Before that.

RICHIE (*Sighs.*) I was just telling you to keep your head down.

EDDIE Oh, I know that.

Richie sighs. Eddie crawls back to the bedroom window

RICHIE Arsehole!

EDDIE I heard that!

Eddie arrives at Rottweiler's bedroom window. Eddie is distracted by something going on in the bedroom. Double take. His eyes pop. He is speechless and nearly falls off. He tries to form words but his mouth is all dry. He turns to Richie and finally gets it together.

EDDIE Bloody hell!

RICHIE Shut up.

EDDIE They're having it off!

RICHIE I'll be right over.

Clatter, clatter, bang, bang. Richie runs along the drainpipe to join Eddie.

From inside the bedroom we see Richie's eager face appear next to Eddie's. He looks.

RICHIE Bloody Hell!

EDDIE You see I told you. You *do* do it like that.

RICHIE God, who'd have thought it? Shove over, I can't see. I can only see one nipple.

The drainpipe creaks.

EDDIE Careful.

RICHIE I want to see some more.

EDDIE Careful.

RICHIE Look!

The drainpipe makes a minor creaking sound.

They drop out of view, then re-appear. Eddie has his instamatic camera. He holds it in one hand.

EDDIE Just get one shot.

Flash! The gutter gives way. They drop completely out of view at speed. We hear lots of clattering below.

SCENE FOUR – STAIRS

RICHIE According to my calculations, Rottweiler's kitchen should be just about . . . here.

He draws a big cross on the wall half way up the stairs.

EDDIE Yeah.

RICHIE So we make a little hole, you squeeze through, fix the gas, and slip out through the front door while I replace the bricks. I mean, what could be simpler than that?

EDDIE Absolutely nothing.

RICHIE You're right and absolutely nothing can go wrong. Right, just take out a couple of bricks here.

He draws a small circle.

EDDIE Okey, dokey matey.

Eddie swings the sledgehammer. Most of the wall collapses. Bricks and dust everywhere.

SCENE FIVE – ROTTWEILER'S BEDROOM

As it clears we see that they have broken into Rottweiler's bedroom, not his kitchen, and that he and his consort, Lolly, are asleep in bed. The boys look startled and rather frightened.

RICHIE Oh well. Despair not.

EDDIE Despair what?

RICHIE Faint heart ne'er won fair maid.

EDDIE (*Looking hard at Richie.*) You talk an incredible amount of bollocks don't you?

RICHIE Shut up! Come on. Sshhh! Sshhh! You go into the kitchen, I'll tidy up in here.

EDDIE Okey dokey.

Eddie steps on squeaky floorboard.

RICHIE Mind the squeaky board.

Eddie steps on the squeaky floorboard again.

EDDIE That one?

RICHIE That's the one.

EDDIE OK.

Eddie exits – stepping on the squeaky floorboard as he goes.

Richie collects up bricks, drops one on Rottweiler's head.

ROTTWEILER Me too.

SCENE SIX – ROTTWEILER'S KITCHEN

Eddie comes into the kitchen. His eyes trace the dayglo green hosepipe from the window down to the meter cupboard which is squeezed in behind the fridge. He starts moving the fridge. The door of the fridge opens. Eddie is surprised to see lots of food in there. He looks around, then takes a sausage.

SCENE SEVEN – BEDROOM

Richie is finishing off his repair work.

RICHIE There!

Richie inspects repair. It is awful. He moves a large chest of drawers to cover the hastily rebuilt wall. It makes loud screeching noises on the floor. Richie keeps looking nervously at the couple on the bed.

SCENE EIGHT – KITCHEN

Eddie has got a plate and is making a meal for himself from the contents of the fridge. He sits down at the table to eat.

SCENE NINE – BEDROOM

Richie pushes the chest of drawers into its final position. It makes a loud screech. Lolly stirs and turns over. Richie can see her cleavage. He goes to the door and whispers loudly towards the kitchen door.

RICHIE How are doing Eddie?

SCENE TEN – KITCHEN/HALLWAY

Eddie speaks through a mouthful of food.

EDDIE Very well thank you.

RICHIE (*Voice off.*) How much longer are you going to be?

Eddie looks at his plateful of food.

EDDIE Ooh, quite a while.

RICHIE I'll just tidy things up in here.

SCENE ELEVEN – BEDROOM

Richie creeps over to the bed and tries to get a peek at Lolly's cleavage. She turns over.

RICHIE No, no, no, no, no!

Richie can't get a good view. He contorts himself into all sorts of positions but it's no good. He decides he'll have to get on to the bed if he wants a proper look. He creeps gingerly onto the squeaky bed, and crawls agonisingly slowly up the bed. When he gets halfway up, Rottweiler farts. Richie coughs a lot.

SCENE TWELVE – KITCHEN

Eddie finishes off his meal with a flourish.

EDDIE Right! Time for a bit of work.

Eddie rolls up his sleeves and looks like he's about to embark on some highly technical work. He grabs the hose and pulls with all his might. It comes out and Eddie falls over backwards into the dresser. It lands on him.

SCENE THIRTEEN – BEDROOM

Richie is more than alarmed at the crescendo of noise coming from the kitchen.

RICHIE Ssshhh!

His eyes dart between Rottweiler and Lolly to see if they wake up. Rottweiler stirs and turns over putting his arm across Richie's neck and his leg across Richie's leg. Richie is trapped. Rottweiler kisses him in his sleep.

SCENE FOURTEEN – KITCHEN

Eddie crudely puts all the broken crockery back onto the dresser.

EDDIE No one would ever know.

Eddie starts to sniff. He looks towards the gas meter. It is obviously leaking gas. He runs over and stops the leak by jamming his finger into the open pipe.

EDDIE Richie!

SCENE FIFTEEN – BEDROOM/LANDING

Richie is still trapped – worse, Rottweiler in his sleep seems to think that Richie is his girlfriend and starts nuzzling him.

RICHIE (*As loudly as his situation decrees, which is barely audible.*) Sssshhhh.

EDDIE (*Voice off.*) Richie!!!!!

RICHIE Oh God. Why didn't we just pay our gas bill?

EDDIE (*Voice off.*) Richie!!!!!!!!!!

RICHIE (*Very quietly but very angrily*) Shut up!

Richie tries to manoeuvre himself. The bed collapses. Lolly screams. There is a jumble of sheets and surprise, during which Richie extricates himself. He ends up at the end of the bed with the sheet over his head.

LOLLY Ooooooh, you really made the earth move you sex monster.

Rottweiler grabs the sheet.

ROTTWEILER Yeah come on, let's do it some more. You raunchy love handle.

Rottweiler jumps back onto the bed.

LOLLY You great hunk of Zebra.

Richie escapes.

SCENE SIXTEEN – STAIRS OUTSIDE KITCHEN

Richie is on the stairs about to enter the kitchen. There is a 'whumpf' of an explosion and the hallway is lit up in front of him.

SCENE SEVENTEEN – KITCHEN

Richie enters the kitchen to see a scarred and bloody Eddie standing next to the meter which has a ten foot jet of flame gushing from it.

RICHIE Eddie, Eddie, what the bloody hell do you think you're doing?

EDDIE (*Nonplussed.*) I thought I'd burn it off.

RICHIE What, your face?

EDDIE No, the excess gas.

RICHIE Oh really? And how long do you think it'll take to burn off the entire North Sea gas reserves?

EDDIE I don't know. What d'you reckon?

RICHIE I reckon we ought to get out of here.

EDDIE Okey dokey, I'll just get rid of the evidence.

Eddie takes the hosepipe and puts it out of the window.

SCENE EIGHTEEN – FRONT DOOR/STAIRWAY/ BEDROOM DOOR

Richie and Eddie run to the front door.

RICHIE Come on, come on. We bloody did it. You and me together. From here to eternity. Come on, let's get out of here.

They open door, gas man is there.

GAS MAN Hello . . . er . . . .

They slam the door.

RICHIE Up the stairs, quick.

They do so – ring on front door.

SCENE NINETEEN – BEDROOM

Richie runs to chest of drawers and squeaks it aside to reveal hole.

RICHIE Give me a hand for Christ's sake.

EDDIE Hang on – one for the album.

Sticks camera under sheets and flashes off shot of Lolly between the sheets – he joins Richie.

SCENE TWENTY – KITCHEN/FRONT DOOR

Rottweiler sees the destruction in his kitchen.

ROTTWEILER Bloody hell – my kitchen. (*Runs to the front door.*) Help, help! Somebody call the Gas Board.

Doorbell rings. He opens the door.

GAS MAN Hello, I'm from the Gas Board.

ROTTWEILER Blimey, that was quick. Look, my kitchen's on fire.

SCENE TWENTY-ONE – KITCHEN

Huge flame in the foreground, the Gas Man and Rottweiler are in the background.

GAS MAN My God! No wonder your gas bill's so high. How did this happen?

ROTTWEILER You tell me face-ache – you're the bleeding expert.

GAS MAN Where are the other two?

ROTTWEILER What other two?

GAS MAN The two loonies from next door. They were here a moment ago.

ROTTWEILER Here in my flat?

GAS MAN Aye, here large as life.

Rottweiler bursts a blood vessel.

SCENE TWENTY-TWO – HALLWAY OF BOYS' FLAT

Eddie and Richie are patting the wall – they are putting the last brick in place.

RICHIE There we are, the last brick – safe and sound at last. I never thought we'd get away with it. Put it right there old pal.

Eddie looks at his groin and thinks.

RICHIE Brains you see Eddie, brains over brawn. I don't expect we'll be seeing Rottweiler for a bit.

Rottweiler's arms smash through the wall and strangle them.

Freeze.

Fin.

BOTTOM CONTEST

SCENE ONE – THE FLAT – KITCHEN

Richie is looking out of the window. It is wet. He sighs. He turns the gas on, opens the oven door and puts his head in. He reaches for a piece of paper and pencil.

Richie signs note. He goes through an elaborate rehearsal of killing himself – putting his head in the oven, taking it out. He acts out the scenario, with himself as Eddie.

RICHIE Right. Eddie comes in. Takes off his coat. Body odour. Takes off his hat. Sits down to eat his tea. Sees the note. Sees me. Shock. Rescue rescue rescue rescue. Remorse remorse. Guilt guilt guilt. Whirlwind of self-loathing and Eddie buys me a drink. Fiendish.

Eddie starts to arrive. We hear his footsteps on the stairs outside. Richie quickly puts his head back into the oven. Eddie enters, he is in a silently furious mood. He slams the door behind him. Almost rips his long gaberdine raincoat as he tears it off and violently thrusts it at the hat stand. He yanks off his hat and throws it straight down at the floor. He sits in his chair with violence, thumping down his bag on top of Richie's note. He withdraws a newspaper from his bag and begins to do the crossword.

Pause.

Richie starts to cough. Eventually Eddie turns round and acknowledges Richie's presence but says nothing. Finally Richie removes his head from the oven, opens the window and wanders over to Eddie.

RICHIE Oh, hello Eddie.

EDDIE Oh bugger off!

RICHIE Hard day at the office?

EDDIE Yes! I spent an hour with Mrs Longbottom. I spent another hour and a half with that bitch Mrs Pugh and then I spent six hours looking for the supervisor's office and, when I got there, he cut off my dole.

RICHIE What?

EDDIE They said I'd got too many savings.

RICHIE Well how much have you got?

EDDIE Eleven pounds eighty. They said that ought to keep me going for at least two months.

RICHIE You really are pathetic, aren't you? I mean you haven't held down a steady job since 1978 and you only held that down for ten minutes. Bunny girl. I told you to keep your trousers on. It was like watching a bull fight. So we've only got eleven pounds eighty to last us for the next two months.

EDDIE No. We've got 30p and a second-hand copy of *Parade*.

RICHIE What?

EDDIE It's an investment. Look, I got it for one pound fifty and originally it only cost a shilling – the value of these things is just sky-rocketing!

RICHIE That's pre-decimalisation, they'll all have their pants on!

Pause.

RICHIE All right, I'd better look after it.

EDDIE Ah, ah, ah, no you don't. This is my investment. I'm going to show this to my grandchildren.

RICHIE I beg your pardon?

EDDIE Look, this is a genuine first edition of *Parade*. It's still in its sealed sellophane wrapper.

RICHIE It doesn't matter how you art it up Eddie, it's still a jazz mag.

EDDIE That's what they said to Michaelangelo about the Sistine Chapel.

RICHIE It is not. The Sistine Chapel is art. If they said anything, they would have said, 'Blimey, nice painting Mr Angelo. Now, that's what I call art, and it's not porny at all'.

EDDIE It bloody well is dirty you know. There's those three birds on the top of the third pillar from the left with that bit of blue ribbon. Cor, some of the things they're doing would make your nose bleed. Here, there's a picture of it in that History of Art book. Where is it?

RICHIE Oh well, let's not bother with all that now Eddie. Let's just have dinner.

EDDIE Ah, there it is, in your study area. That's odd, it's fallen open at the exact page.

Eddie lets the book fall open again.

EDDIE Extraordinary. It's done it again.

Eddie does it again.

RICHIE Yes, well I've been studying that picture.

EDDIE Been studying it quite a lot have you? While you're alone in the house?

RICHIE How dare you accuse me of masturbating.

EDDIE Who said anything about masturbating?

RICHIE You did, just then.

EDDIE I did not. I just said it's odd how it always falls open at that precise page.

RICHIE Yes you did and the reason you said that is because you know that's the picture I always look at when I'm having a w....

Richie's eyes swivel as he realises he's admitted to something that he shouldn't.

Pause.

RICHIE Eleven pounds eighty was all we had to survive on for the next two months. I mean, what am I going to feed the children on now?

EDDIE We haven't got any children.

RICHIE Yes, I know, I know. I'm talking metaphorically.

EDDIE You're talking bollocks.

RICHIE Don't you go using language like that in my house my lad.

EDDIE What? English?

RICHIE The language of the guttersnipe, the language of the, of the toilet, the language of the little green things you give a big yank to and you get a big yellow bit coming out . . . .

EDDIE Oh God! Shut up! Every day yakkety bloody yak, on and on and on, day in day out, slime in this ear, slime in that ear, just stop talking.

Richie looks hurt. Sulkily he starts laying the tea. Eddie breaks his model plane.

RICHIE You may hate me Eddie.

EDDIE Yes, I do.

RICHIE But you can't live without me can you? I mean, off you go gallivanting around the countryside, squandering all our money on rhythm magazines and then you come swanning in here and expect to have your dinner on the table . . . and I don't know why I do it, but I've managed to throw together a slap-up dinner for two for no money at all. All the ingredients in tonight's main meal have either been grown, found or foraged.

EDDIE Oh dear.

RICHIE So hey. Hey. Hey. Eddie. I forgive you. Come and have yer din-dins.

Richie gets both plates of food and dribbles on one. He places the plates on the table indicating that Eddie should eat the dribbled on food. Eddie takes a place by the other food. Richie curses to himself.

EDDIE What's wrong with these beans?

RICHIE What do you mean wrong? They're fresh. I grew those in the window box. I've decided for the very highest moral and ecological reasons that we are going to be vegetarians.

EDDIE What, were you banned from the butchers *again*?

RICHIE Yeah, and the greengrocers – but it's amazing what you can find in the park.

EDDIE But they've got black bits all over them.

RICHIE Well it's just a couple of greenfly for heaven's sake. But they're dead now, they've been under the grill for ages. Really – I watched them pop.

Eddie roots around in his food. Picks something up on his fork. It's radish-sized.

EDDIE What's this?

RICHIE It's a turnip. What are you missing – the label?

EDDIE Why's it black?

RICHIE (*Exasperated.*) It's been grilled!!!

Richie eats. It is terrible. He gamely pretends to enjoy it.

RICHIE They have a real texture don't they? Fresh vegetables. It's a totally different experience.

EDDIE Grilled lettuce?

RICHIE No, that's bacon.

EDDIE It's green!

RICHIE Yeah!

EDDIE I can't eat this, it's disgusting.

RICHIE Well what are you going to do then, Egon Ronay? Blow your thirty pence on a slap-up grill down the Savoy?

Eddie looks almost imperceptibly shifty.

EDDIE Pass the tea.

Richie pours him a cup. It's muddy coloured water. Eddie looks none too pleased.

EDDIE What's this?

RICHIE Elm tea. (*Slight pause.*) The gypsies swear by it.

EDDIE I bet they do! I bet they say, 'What the bloody hell's this?'

RICHIE God, it's like living with Lena Zavaroni.

Richie takes a sip of his tea and gags.

RICHIE You can taste the bark, can't you? Perhaps a little less wood next time.

EDDIE Is there any pudding?

RICHIE Oh yes. Plenty of pud.

Eddie gets up walks towards the TV.

EDDIE Right! I'm off. At least there's something fantastic on telly tonight. I've been looking forward to this for ages.

Eddie turns the TV on.

RICHIE You can't watch that actually.

Richie switches channels.

EDDIE And why not?

RICHIE 'Cos there's something *I* want to watch on the other side. It's my favourite programme.

EDDIE This is your favourite programme?

RICHIE Yes.

EDDIE What is it?

Richie doesn't know.

RICHIE It's a documentary.

Pause.

And there's a car – great. Yeah look, it's a documentary about fat old women.

EDDIE What, are you in it then?

RICHIE What? Oh ha ha. Oh yeah hysterical Eddie, heart stoppingly funny. You really should be on Channel 4.

EDDIE No, ITV, that's the channel for me, nothing to worry about and plenty of sauce.

RICHIE Really, and what particularly edifying programme have the light channel prepared for us this evening that I'm not going to let us watch?

EDDIE It's *Miss World* actually.

RICHIE How disgusting.

(*To himself.*)

Shit!

They both sit and watch for a bit.

ANNOUNCER . . . precision of the measurement of aggregate change . . . .

RICHIE Oooh. Nice statistic.

ANNOUNCER . . . cross-section and the higher the correlation . . . .

Click. Eddie has turned the TV over to Miss World.

MISS SPAIN My hobbies are flower arranging and meeting people . . . .

EDDIE Cor!!

Click. Richie turns it back.

ANNOUNCER . . . cross-section study can monitor change at an individual level by asking . . . .

Click. Eddie and Richie turn it over and over in succession getting quicker and quicker, whilst trying to stop each other getting to the buttons. Eventually they manage to knock the TV over onto its back. Richie loses his temper.

RICHIE Right. That's it. Get out of my house.

EDDIE I beg your pardon.

RICHIE You heard.

EDDIE No I didn't.

RICHIE Well I'm not saying something like that twice young man.

EDDIE Well, I can't do anything about it then can I?

RICHIE Look, this is my house, so get out.

EDDIE You can't throw me out just like that, I've got rights, I pay rent.

RICHIE You're supposed to pay rent. I've never actually seen any money.

EDDIE Well, I've been busy, haven't I? How much is it?

RICHIE To date: eleven thousand, six hundred and forty five pounds and sixty six new pence.

EDDIE I've got 30p.

RICHIE You'd better get out of my house then hadn't you?

EDDIE It's not your house. It's your aunt's house.

RICHIE For the purposes of this conversation, I am my aunt.

EDDIE Hello Mabel.

RICHIE (*Panic.*) What, is she here? Shit. Hide the fags! Hello Auntie! (*Realises his mistake.*) Right, that's it. Get out!

Eddie puts on his hat and coat.

EDDIE Right, I shall go, Mabel. But I think I ought to warn you that if your nephew reads any more art magazines he very well may go blind. Good day to you madam.

Eddie exits.

RICHIE Good riddance to bad rubbish. That was clever.

We see Eddie outside in the corridor.

Richie rights the TV and furtively switches it on to Miss World. He starts getting sexy.

ANNOUNCER So let's meet our ten semi-finalists in their swimwear. First will you please greet number 16, Miss Dominican Republic. (*Cheering.*) Maria is only 19 years old . . . .

Cut to outside corridor.

EDDIE (*To himself.*) I'm very sorry, Richie. You're the tops. Let's have another cup of that delicious elm tea. Ah well it's either that or Nasty Linda. Eeugh.

Eddie enters room. He is just about to speak and stops. He sees Richie with his trousers down beginning to get very amorous with himself. Eddie walks very slowly over to Richie. Richie does not notice. Eddie coughs.

RICHIE Sssh!

Richie suddenly realises Eddie is there and pulls his trousers up. Switches back to the documentary.

EDDIE Oh dear, this isn't very sexy is it?

Pause.

EDDIE Cor, look at the knockers on that one, they're minute!

RICHIE That's because that's Michael Buerk.

Pause.

EDDIE Well, he's not very saucy is he? I mean I'm all for educational programmes – I just think they could, you know, sex them up a bit. What do you think, Richie?

They laugh.

RICHIE This is all so silly. I mean just because the television set got jammed onto the light channel during the fall and at precisely the same moment my trousers accidentally fell down due to heavy housework . . . .

EDDIE Richie . . . .

RICHIE . . . is no reason . . . .

EDDIE Richie, don't even try it. Just put the TV back on to *Miss World* and we'll say no more about it.

RICHIE We'll say no more about it?

EDDIE No.

Richie turns the TV back on to Miss World.

RICHIE Thanks.

EDDIE Now go away.

RICHIE I'll just go away over here. In my going away place. And here I am in my going away place, on my own. Well, it's a bit of a loose end for me really. So I'll just tidy away the dinner things. Yes, just tidy away the dinner that I cooked and nobody ate. I'll just throw away the vegetables (*he scrapes the plates out of the window*) . . . onto that man – all the vegetables I spent all day grilling. Off they go and I'm sure that God's looking down, thinking, 'What a good ecological . . . .'

EDDIE Richard, I'm warning you. If you don't shut up and let me watch *Miss World*, I'm going to stuff your head up your bum, and you'll spend the rest of your life wandering about on all fours looking for the light switch.

Eddie settles down to watch Miss World *making the occasional 'cor' noise.*

RICHIE OK, I'll have a cup of tea.

Richie pours himself a cup of elm tea and carries it to the organ. He sits at the organ and accidentally switches on to one of the auto-rhythm thingies. It takes him a few dangerous seconds and tuneless chords to work out how to switch it off. Relief.

RICHIE God, they don't write tunes like that any more.

Richie mooches over to join Eddie.

RICHIE It's just I, I'm just a very lonely person Eddie.

EDDIE I'm not bloody surprised.

Richie watches TV.

RICHIE Oh. Great. *Miss World*. Cor – cracking birds, aren't they? Do you know how many birds there are in the world?

EDDIE Yeah. About three billion.

RICHIE And do you know how many of those I've slept with?

EDDIE Yes.

RICHIE None.

EDDIE Yeah, I know.

RICHIE I mean, statistically that's really quite phenomenal, isn't it?

EDDIE Not for an ugly fat bastard like you.

RICHIE That's what I'm missing from life.

EDDIE What, a quick nasty?

RICHIE No Eddie, love. The love of a good woman. An English rose. A Scottish heather. A Welsh . . . dragon.

EDDIE A German sausage.

RICHIE Yeah, an Irish . . . wolfhound.

EDDIE A Chinese takeaway.

RICHIE A Spanish . . . omelette – any of those'd do for me, except the Irish wolfhound obviously.

EDDIE But all right with a German sausage then?

RICHIE All right Eddie, let's skim over the details, it's only a metaphor. Give him an inch he makes a porn movie. Tcch. (*Sighs.*) Why haven't I got a girlfriend? I wish I had a girlfriend – it'd be someone to listen to me. All I've got is you Eddie.

EDDIE Careful.

RICHIE I wonder what sort of great bird'd suit me.

EDDIE A blind one. Blind deaf masochist really.

RICHIE Yeah. I suppose you're right. I mean me, you know . . . I was born at the wrong time you see. I'm more sort of Elizabethan, you know, thirteenth century, Shakespeare, the French Revolution, all that. I'm just too intelligent, that's my problem.

He leans on the kettle.

RICHIE Ooh, shit, ow! I didn't expect the kettle to be hot. God – life's horrible. Why haven't I got a girlfriend? I'd look great with a girlfriend – I've never had a girlfriend.

He runs his hand under the cold tap.

RICHIE Perhaps I'm the new Messiah! Yeah, maybe that's it. 'Get up and walk.' 'Fifty quid.' 'Throw away your sticks.' Bonk. 'April Fool! Ha ha!' Oh God I'm bored. Oh! There's the phone . . . we haven't had a phone conversation all night Eddie. I'm great on the phone.

He picks it up.

RICHIE Hello . . . Great! Hi! . . . Greater.

Puts the phone down then picks it up again.

Lieutentant Sex Machine, homicide. Yeah, what time? Damn! I'm going to nail this sick mother even if the DA takes my badge. Chief, just give me 24 hours.

Throws the phone down on the receiver and reflects with awe.

Oh God, I wish I knew what all that meant . . . 'Dring, dring. Dring, dring'.

He snatches the phone up.

RICHIE Hello, look who is this? Just don't hurt the kid OK?

Puts his hand over the receiver and talks to Eddie.

Eddie. Eddie. It's him again, he's got Janie, switch on the tape recorder. How much do you want? Fourteen million billion squillion zillion dollars? What, are you crazy? Oh, you are . . . Sorry. 'Scuse me. Well where am I going to get fourteen million billion squillion zillion dollars? We've only got 30p. Eddie blew the rest on a second-hand copy of *Parade*!

He puts the phone down.

Hang on.

Richie walks over to the TV and turns it off.

Eddie reacts.

You had eleven pounds eighty, right? You spent one pound fifty on the porn mag.

EDDIE Art pamphlet.

RICHIE That is beside the point. One pound fifty from eleven pounds eighty leaves ten pounds thirty and you've only got 30p. Where's the other tenner you grasping little Fagin?

EDDIE Oh sod off, you stupid fat git.

RICHIE Don't try and wriggle out of it by being all grown-up. What did you squander it on?

EDDIE I put a bet on *Miss World*.

RICHIE You put a bet on *Miss World*? You put a bet on *Miss World*?! Great!

He switches the TV back on and they both sit back rubbing their hands with glee and making lewd noises.

EDDIE Richie. Richie. This is *Panorama*.

He scrabbles frantically to switch the TV over.

RICHIE Great, which one's ours old chum?

EDDIE Miss China.

RICHIE Miss China. All right, where are you my lovely?

EDDIE There she is! There she is!

Richie spots her. Face aghast.

RICHIE Eddie, you haven't put our money on that old boiler have you?

EDDIE Go on me beauty, mind the steps – ooh, that's a bit of a nasty tumble.

RICHIE She can't even walk!

EDDIE She's lost a couple of teeth. Spit 'em out dear, they'll never notice.

RICHIE Well stop smiling you stupid cow. Gawd look at her mouth, there should be a lollipop man standing on it, stopping the traffic. Eddie what on earth possessed you to put our money on the thing from the swamp?

EDDIE I got odds on a thousand to one. If she comes in ahead of the pack, we stand to make ten thousand quid. Oh imagine it, lying on the sun-drenched shore as the Caribbean laps at your feet, a scantily clad maiden brings you your seventeenth large tequila sunrise and a slap-up grill for two.

RICHIE Well the way Quasimodo's going, we'll be lucky to get a wet weekend in Reigate.

Shouts at the screen.

She's got a tattoo on her face!

EDDIE No, that's just a bit of blood.

RICHIE Oh Eddie, why couldn't you put our money on something decent like Miss America?

EDDIE Pointless Richie, the odds were five to one on, we'd have only made two quid.

RICHIE Well two quid in the hand is better than a tenner down the lav. What's wrong with the reception?

EDDIE Well it's your fault for knocking the telly over. Hang on, I'll give it a bang.

Eddie fixes the TV with an idiosyncratic slap.

ANNOUNCER Well a shame about the fall there Shin Tei, I hope there's not too much damage, and I'm sure the judges will take that into account. Now tell me – from what part of lovely China do you come from?

The sound fizzles and becomes unintelligible.

RICHIE I can't make out a word of this.

EDDIE Well that's because she's talking in Chinese.

RICHIE Hang on, I'll give it a bang.

He tries to repeat Eddie's idiosyncratic slap. Telly goes off immediately.

EDDIE You stupid git, there's ten grand riding on this.

RICHIE I'm sorry.

Eddie fixes the TV with another slap.

RICHIE How do you do that?

He tries it again and the set explodes and the lights go out.

EDDIE Richie, are you all right? Where are you?

RICHIE I'm over the other side of the room.

EDDIE Over here?

RICHIE No, over here.

EDDIE Over here?

RICHIE No, this is me here.

Sound of enormous punch.

EDDIE Now, did we get any more fuse wire?

RICHIE It's in the kitchen drawer.

They stumble through to the kitchen, knocking over the furniture as they go. Fumble in the drawer.

EDDIE There's nothing in here.

RICHIE That's 'cos that's the fridge . . . Ooh shit, mind the kettle, it's still hot.

EDDIE Where is it?

RICHIE It's down here. Ooh shit, I've done it again, that's three times now.

EDDIE Oh God, there's no fuse wire in here. Richie?

RICHIE What?

EDDIE Get up here and hold this.

RICHIE What?

The lights snap on and flicker erratically and we see Richie on the top of a stepladder holding a screwdriver jammed into the fuse box. It's flashing and sparking. He occasionally gets a shock. The TV comes on. There is a drum roll.

ANNOUNCER And in third place, is number forty-two, Miss Guava!

We hear cheering, then everything blacks out as Richie pulls away from the fuse box.

EDDIE Stick it back in! Stick it back in! We're seconds away from the result.

RICHIE No Eddie, please.

The lights snap on again to reveal Eddie pushing Richie's hand back into the fuse box. The TV comes back on.

ANNOUNCER And in second place, number twelve, Miss America!

Huge cheering. Eddie rushes over to the set and watches intently.

EDDIE Heh Richie! That was Miss America, the favourite! We're in with a chance!

RICHIE I think I'm going to faint.

EDDIE Yeah, it is pretty exciting isn't it?

The fuse box is beginning to spark more than usual. Reception on the TV fades in and out.

RICHIE Eddie, I can't hold it much longer.

EDDIE Another ten seconds.

RICHIE Please, it's your turn, surely it's your turn!

EDDIE Oh, shut your cakehole.

ANNOUNCER And the winner of this year's Miss World is . . . .

Drum roll.

RICHIE Go on, have a go Eddie. It's fun!

EDDIE Here it comes.

ANNOUNCER . . . number thirty-seven, Miss France!!

EDDIE I don't believe it! It's a fix.

RICHIE Did we win?

EDDIE No, we lost.

RICHIE Knackers!

The fuse box and the TV explode. The lights go out. In the gloom we see Richie fall from the ladder.

EDDIE Richie, are you OK?

RICHIE Am I OK? No I'm not bloody OK. Wait till I get my hands on you, you little bastard. Oooh shit! That bloody kettle's still hot. Oh God, life's horrible – ten grand down the toilet and a scalded hand. Why does fate treat me like this? Ah well, at least things can't get any worse.

We can see Richie silhouetted against the gloom of the back window. He stumbles about trying to find Eddie and falls silently out of the open window. We hear him hit the dustbins below. A dog yelps.

The lights come on and Eddie is revealed at the top of the ladder having fixed the lights.

EDDIE There we go. Dab hand Eddie. That'll be eleven thousand, six hundred and forty five pounds and sixty-six new pence. Or we could just call it quits on the rent, Richie, Richie? Richie?

Pause.

I'll take that as a 'yes' then, shall I?

He spots the fake suicide note Richie wrote earlier.

EDDIE (*Reads.*) 'Dear Eddie, by the time you read this, I will be dead. I know you will be feeling terribly guilty but don't blame yourself. Although it really is your fault. If I was alive I would forgive you, but I'm not, so I can't, so you'll just have to live with it. Richard.'

Finishes reading and lowers the note.

EDDIE Poor blighter. All he needed was the love of a good woman, well, not even a good one, any old one would have done. Slap a wig on a Speak-Your-Weight machine and he'd have been happy. And now he's gone and done himself in.

Pause.

Eddie wanders over to the organ and leans on it.

EDDIE Well this ought to fetch a few quid.

Richie enters.

RICHIE Who left the kitchen window open?

EDDIE Richie! You're alive!

RICHIE Yes. The amount of pain I'm in would suggest so.

EDDIE Oh dear. All right, well hang on then, I'll get you a bandaid.

RICHIE Take your time Mother Teresa!

Richie goes straight to the phone and dials.

RICHIE Hello BBC? Put me through to the *Miss World* programme. I wish to complain in the strongest possible terms . . . Yeah? Well put me through to ITV then . . . Hello? Hello? Would you believe it?

Slams the phone down.

RICHIE It's just typical isn't it? We're on the brink of winning ten thousand pounds, and some ugly frog bint scoops up all our hopes in her garlic-stained claw and discards them like some used tissue.

EDDIE That's very poetic Richie.

RICHIE Oh sod off! Go on, sod off! Get to soddery! It's all your fault!

EDDIE Sod off yourself, you great fat git! It's me that's just lost ten thousand quid.

RICHIE Well half of it was mine.

EDDIE It bloody well was not! Do you think I'm going to lie around the sun-drenched Caribbean with bus-fulls of dusky maidens fulfilling every sordid whim and have a great fat blotchy white walrus lying next to me blabbering on and on about himself and spoiling the atmos? No, I'm bloody not.

RICHIE Well thank you very much, Edward. You learn something every day, don't you? And today I learned that you're a complete bastard. Well I think I might turn in now, I feel so enriched. Nighty, night Eddie.

He heads for the bedroom door. Then gets angry and turns back.

Why can't we ever bloody win anything?

EDDIE Oh don't be stupid, Richie. People like us aren't meant to win things.

RICHIE Well, what are we meant to do then?

EDDIE Look, you get born, you keep your head down, and then you die. If you're lucky.

RICHIE Oh come on Eddie, there must be more to it than that.

EDDIE Well, there's the telly – well there was.

Richie sighs.

EDDIE Do you want me to switch the gas on?

RICHIE What do you mean?

EDDIE Go on – top yourself. The telly's bust. It'd be a good bit of entertainment.

RICHIE Ha ha. I know you're just trying to cheer me up. And you're right, you know. You have to laugh don't you? (*Sour face.*) No, you don't really, do you? It's no good, I think I've reached my bottom. What we couldn't have done with ten thousand grand.

EDDIE Well we couldn't have done anything really. You see, I never put the bet on – I just said I did so that you'd insist we watched *Miss World*.

Richie looks hard at him for a moment.

RICHIE Well where's the missing tenner then?

EDDIE Well, I saw you picking your veg as I went out this morning, so I thought I'd better have a slap-up grill before I came home. Yum yum!

Richie hits Eddie.

Freeze.

Fin.

BOTTOM APOCALYPSE

SCENE ONE – LIVING ROOM

Dead goldfish is floating in bowl.

RICHIE Is it dead?

EDDIE Yeah.

RICHIE Right, shall we fry it or poach it?

EDDIE I don't really care as long as I get the head.

RICHIE Right, this is definitely the only food in the house?

EDDIE That's right, the rest is hidden in the cistern.

RICHIE Right, so we bring her in, we sit her down and she sees that we're so poor that we've had to kill Elvis just to give her something for her tea.

EDDIE Yeah.

RICHIE She's very fond of animals Eddie, that's why it's so important that you're here.

EDDIE Right.

RICHIE And if that doesn't break her heart . . . .

EDDIE Then this will. (*Holds up cosh.*)

RICHIE No, Eddie, no.

EDDIE Oh come on Richie, let's just rumble the old bird?

HAMMERSMITH & FULHAM
ERSMITH
ROAD W.6    
LOND
Limit
ons
nith Bridge

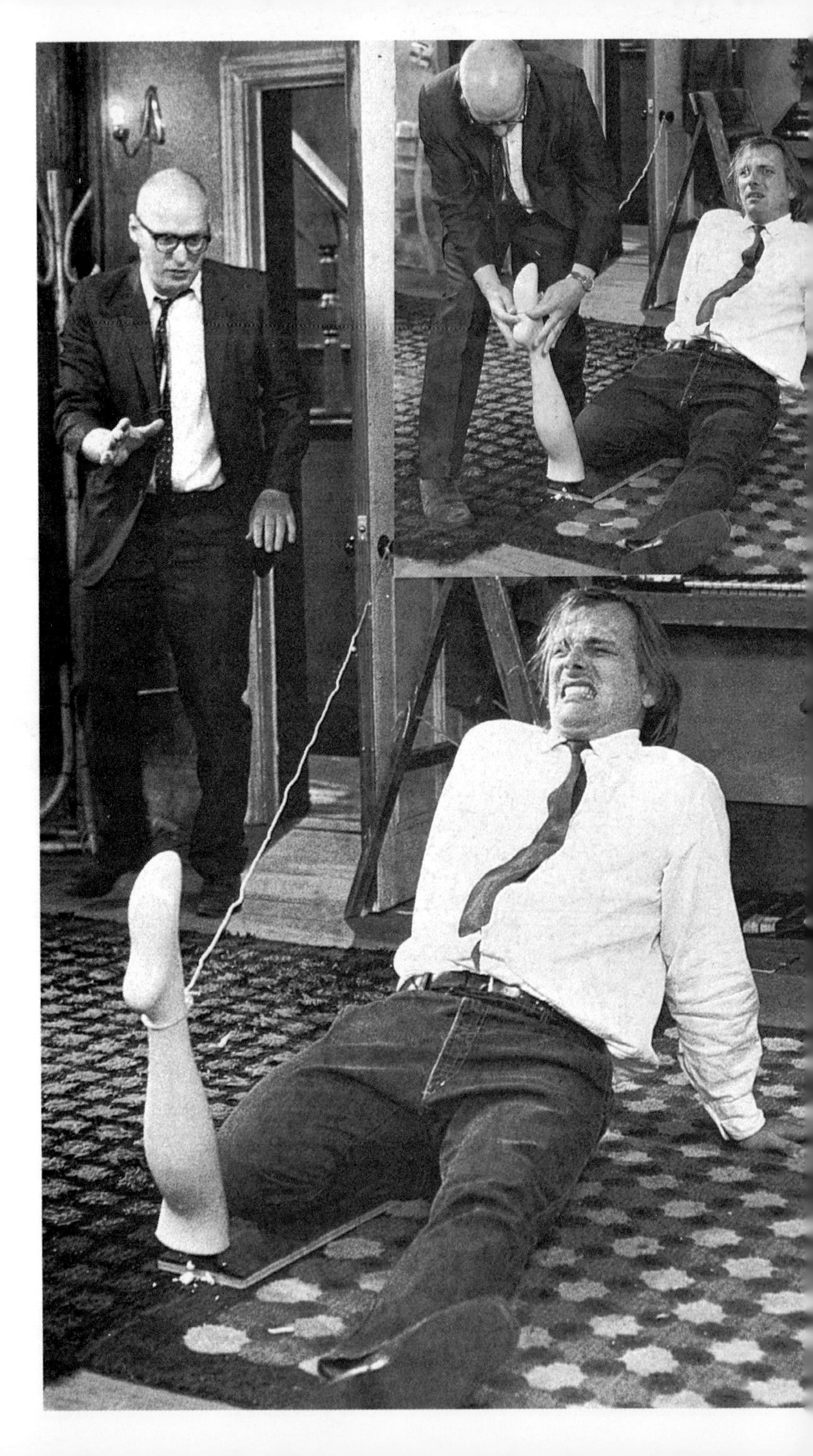

RICHIE Look. We've got gas bills, we've got electric bills, we've got poll tax and we've got rent. Our only chance is to get Auntie Olga to write us a big fat cheque. Ooh, that reminds me. I'd better get her to bring all her cheque books. (*Goes to phone.*) Daft old cow brought a bunch of bananas last time. Eddie, spread those bills around strategically so she sees one wherever she sits.

(*To phone.*) Hello operator. Yeah, I'd like to make a reverse charge call, please. Little Piddle 338.

(*To Eddie.*) Eddie, you know what you've got to say when she gets here.

EDDIE Yeah. Eh – give us some money you old bag.

RICHIE No!

EDDIE Give us some money you old witch.

RICHIE No!

EDDIE Old bastard?

RICHIE No!

EDDIE Git?

RICHIE No, you say 'I am a sad orphan'.

EDDIE Right. I am a sad orphan. Give us some money you old bag.

RICHIE (*To phone.*) No you pratt. Oh no . . . hello operator, not you . . . ha ha ha. Yeah? Well tell them it's Richard Richard . . . Yes. Eddie . . . Eddie . . . sprinkle some water about the place to make it look like we've been crying a lot. . . . What do you mean they won't accept the charges? Bastards. (*Slams down phone.*) I'm going to have to dial direct.

EDDIE (*Holding up a bill.*) What's this? Annual membership to Barbarella's aerobic fitness centre.

RICHIE Nothing to do with me.

EDDIE It's got Richard Richard written on it.

RICHIE Ah . . . Er . . . .

EDDIE Leotard?

RICHIE Well Eddie, none of us are getting any younger, I just pop along every Wednesday afternoon and firm up.

EDDIE What – you stand at the back of a room full of girls jiggling their bottoms up and down and firm up?

RICHIE That's right.

EDDIE I bet you do.

RICHIE Listen you big fat . . . ooh hello Auntie, it's Ricky Ticky Tavey . . . Kissy kissy kissy, hug hug hug . . . oh it's you Mrs Higginbottom, you sad old fart, go and get my Auntie . . . What do you mean – no? You're still a servant aren't you? Do what you're bloody told. Get that zimmer cracking. Shut up! Shut up! I still remember what I saw when I was four. Yeah – you, the chauffeur, the bucket of fish – yeah, so go and get her . . . I don't care if she's dead, just go and get . . . What? Eddie! My Auntie's dead. When did it happen? Last night? Mmmm. So they haven't read the will yet. Go and get it . . . Well look in the desk . . . Well search the body then, and hands off those gold teeth – I've got first dibs on them.

EDDIE (*Into phone.*) I'm a sad orphan. Give us your gold teeth you old bitch.

RICHIE Shut up! This is a very difficult time for me . . . Have you got it? Great ! What does it say? Fantastic!

SCENE TWO – FAIRGROUND

Eddie and Richie are in the fairground shooting gallery. Eddie is twirling the rifle round and round in his fingers and shooting at all the prizes instead of the targets. Richie is in a fabulous mood.

RICHIE The little duckling, get the little duckling.

Eddie shoots the duckling.

RICHIE That's right. Blaze away Eddie, blaze away. We deserve a little celebration – Auntie Olga is dead at last! Six hundred smackers to do whatever we like with. Three hundred pounds right here. (*Waving it about.*) And three hundred more safe and sound on top of the bathroom cabinet where no one will ever find them.

Other punters listen with interest as Richie stuffs his wallet into his pocket. The man from the shooting gallery comes up to Eddie.

EDDIE Right, well I'll have another one hundred bullets please mate.

MAN Hold it! That's forty-five quid you owe me so far.

EDDIE Ah. I haven't got any money.

The man grabs Eddie.

RICHIE N-n-n-no. No need for that. I'll get the forty-five quid. Oh I love you Romany types with your legendary campfire hospitality and your quaint insistence on settling bills immediately . . . .

Realises his wallet's gone.

RICHIE Thieving bastard gypos! Someone's swiped my wallet!

MAN Yeah, a likely story. Come on, I want my forty-five quid!

RICHIE Did you not hear what I just said? I've just lost three hundred pounds! Yeah, and I wouldn't be surprised if it was you that nicked it you swarthy thieving nomad. Yeah, either you or one of your slippery deformed half-brothers. Yes, yes! I know what you gypsies get up to when the lights go out . . . 'Extended family'? It's just another word for a sexual free-for-all. Well you're not in Romania now buster and I'm going to go and get a British policeman.

He makes to go. The man picks up a gun and turns it on Richie. Richie immediately sticks his hands up.

MAN You are going nowhere till I get my forty-five quid.

RICHIE Eddie! Help!

EDDIE Em . . . Why don't you give me another crack at the fifty quid star prize, and we'll call it double or quits.

MAN Yeah. All right.

RICHIE (*Sighs.*) Good luck Eddie . . .

Eddie takes careful aim.

EDDIE Em, 'scuse me mate.

MAN Yeah?

The man turns and Eddie shoots him in the eye.

Richie and Eddie make a run for it, pursued by burly fairground workers. They run into Brenda the Ballgazer's tent.

SCENE THREE – BRENDA'S TENT

The boys enter panting.

RICHIE Three hundred quid! Thieving bastard vagabonds.

The voice of an old woman comes from behind them.

BRENDA Cross my palm with silver.

Richie and Eddie turn to see an old woman in traditional fortune-teller's gear, sitting behind a table with a crystal ball on it.

RICHIE Oh my God, there's another one!

BRENDA Cross my palm with silver.

RICHIE No I will not. You and your lot have had more than enough off me today, thank you very much.

BRENDA Then you must leave the tent.

RICHIE Nothing would give me a greater pleasure. (*To Eddie who is looking through the flap.*) How's it look Eddie?

EDDIE Well on a scale of one to ten, I'd say it's bicycle-clip time.

RICHIE Damn! All right then you old battleaxe, you may read me my fortune.

BRENDA First you must cross my palm with silver.

RICHIE Look I can't cross your palm with silver, I've just had my wallet nicked. You're a fortune teller – you should know that.

BRENDA Cross my palm with silver.

RICHIE But I've only got five pee left.

BRENDA That's not enough.

RICHIE Give me strength! Look can't you criss-cross it about the place a bit?

BRENDA It's not enough.

RICHIE Well just give me five pence worth then, we know you get it all from the *Evening Standard* anyway.

BRENDA (*Breaking out of her foreign accent.*) For five pee your future's going to look pretty bleak, mate.

RICHIE Have you got a licence for what you do? I bet you haven't have you? I think either you give me a free fortune telling or I'll phone the police and tell them. Yeah, and they'll deport you back to Umma Gumma land or wherever it is you come from. You'll eke out the rest of your days making little elephants from bits of dried banana.

BRENDA Yes I have got a licence. Unlike you.

Pause. Richie turns.

BRENDA Your driving licence is a fake.

RICHIE How do you know that? Eddie, maybe the old crone's got something.

EDDIE Yeah, looks like dropsy.

BRENDA At least my licence doesn't say 'Martin Andrews' crossed out, and 'Sir Richard Richard VC' crudely written over the top of the plastic in biro.

RICHIE How do you know these things?

BRENDA I see everything.

RICHIE What else do you see?

BRENDA I see . . . ooh, ooh . . . I see a naughty nudey picture of a little lady, with Julia Somerville's face plastered on top of it.

RICHIE Bloody hell Eddie, that's my secret love picture that nobody knows about. She's a genius.

EDDIE Yeah. Hey ask her if she can see a picture of Julia Somerville with her own body all nudey.

RICHIE Shut up Eddie.

EDDIE . . . and whether we can get a copy of it. Be worth a fortune that.

RICHIE I think the crone might be worth a fortune. Tell me more old bag.

BRENDA I cannot tell you more without more money.

RICHIE But I haven't got any more money.

BRENDA Well give me your watch.

RICHIE All right. Here you are.

Brenda makes mystical 'mmmmms' and 'ahhs'.

BRENDA Before the moon rises three times . . . .

RICHIE Yes?

BRENDA . . . you're going to die.

RICHIE I'm going to . . . What?!

BRENDA You are going to die.

RICHIE No no.

BRENDA The power is fading . . . .

RICHIE Here, let me have a look.

BRENDA The orb is dimming.

RICHIE Cor what a swizz.

BRENDA Well what do you expect for five pence?

RICHIE And my watch!

BRENDA It's broken.

RICHIE Hhhhh!!! She's a genius!

SCENE FOUR – HOSPITAL SURGERY

Richie and Eddie come up some stairs and moan at the lift which has an out of order sign on it. Richie walks on up to the counter pushing past all the old sick people.

RICHIE Come on Eddie, oh God. Oh God. Bloody NHS. They put reception on the top floor and keep the lifts out of order just to drum up a bit of heart attack business.

EDDIE Come on Richie, you're taking this far too seriously. The shifty old witch was only having a bit of a joke.

RICHIE She was right about the nudey pic. Oh, how all my sins do inform against me! Come on, come on. Out the way! Out the way! Out the way. Look, are you terminal?

Pushes man on zimmer frame onto floor and speaks to nurse at the counter.

RICHIE Come on. Come on. I want to see a doctor.

NURSE Do you have an appointment?

RICHIE Of course I have an appointment.

NURSE What's your name?

Richie leans over the counter to read the appointment book.

RICHIE Er, Williams.

NURSE Oh Mr Williams, goodness gracious you *are* looking well.

RICHIE Well you know, I like to put a brave face on it. One doesn't like to wallow in these things . . . .

NURSE Yes, and you've grown two new legs.

RICHIE Yeah, they're great . . . (*Looking across at the book again.*) No, no, not Williams, that other name that sounds like Williams. There it is – Henderson. I always get those ones mixed up.

NURSE That's even more remarkable, *Mr* Henderson – you died at six o'clock this morning, and you've changed sex.

RICHIE All right Poirot, so I haven't got an appointment.

NURSE Why didn't you make an appointment?

RICHIE Because I didn't know I was going to be ill.

NURSE I'm sorry sir, but unless it's an emergency.

RICHIE It is, it is, it's an emergency.

NURSE Why, what's the matter?

RICHIE I've only got three days to live.

NURSE Why, what's wrong with you?

RICHIE I don't know.

NURSE Well how do you feel?

RICHIE I feel great.

NURSE Look. There's some genuinely sick people in here who need attention . . . .

RICHIE Yeah, and I think you're one of them Mrs.

NURSE I can book you in a week next Friday.

RICHIE So this is it is it? This is the land fit for heroes. I hurt my leg in the Falklands conflict for this did I?

OLD PATIENT (*To Eddie.*) Did he?

EDDIE Oh yeah. Yeah. He tripped over the coffee table trying to switch channels. Really nasty gash. Kept the plaster on for days.

RICHIE Well, it's just not good enough. I pay my taxes . . . well, well that's not important. I demand to see a doctor right now. What's the matter – are they all round the back flogging off the morphine?

A doctor pokes his head out of one of the cubicles. He is wearing the robes of a surgeon.

DOCTOR Look, I've got a dying woman in here, will you shut up and get out? You look perfectly well to me.

RICHIE Perfectly well? Look buster, if I'd wanted a transvestite's opinion, I'd have gone to the Whisky-a-Go-Go. I'm here to see a doctor.

DOCTOR Do you mind, I'm Sir Roger Cobham OBE, the world-famous heart surgeon. This is my hospital. Now then. (*Examines him.*) You look perfectly well to me. Shut up and get out!

The doctor goes back behind the screen to his patient.

RICHIE Thank God. (*Richie follows the doctor.*) Sorry I didn't recognise you there Doc, I've got bad eye sight you see. It was a Falklands war wound.

He leans on the patient and blood spurts over the doctor.

Sorry about that. Anyway, thanks again mate.

He goes back into the waiting room, then returns to the doctor.

Well look, is there anything I can do to help? I mean, I owe you one now. Anything you want, just name it. You want spare parts, look I've got Eddie right here. Anything I can do to help, you just name it mate.

DOCTOR I want you to stop talking and leave this hospital.

RICHIE You got it. We're outta here.

He starts to go back into the waiting room.

Come on, Eddie – you heard the man.

He goes back in beside the doctor.

Come on, come on . . . .

He slaps the doctor on the back and his face falls into the blood.

90 Sorry, sorry. Look, I know the National Health Service – have a quid, go on. Oh, I haven't got any money. Well, I'll owe it to you, alright. Thanks again mate. (*Turns to patient.*) And thanks to you too dear. (*To doctor.*) Should she really be that colour?

DOCTOR Get out!

RICHIE Right, well there we are Eddie. See you all later. Ha ha ha.

He crosses to the nurse and pats her face, smearing it with blood.

Thanks dear, doing a great job. Oh sorry. There you are, Eddie – a clean bill of health. See, I knew the old crone was insane. Oooh great, the lift's working again.

The lift arrives and, just to prove he's nice, when the doors 'ping', he pushes a little old man in a wheelchair in first.

RICHIE Ah, it's good to be alive. After you, old timer.

The man disappears down the lift shaft.

MAN Aggggghhhhh!!!

Richie looks after him aghast. He turns to Eddie ashen-faced.

RICHIE God. That's terrible . . . that could have been me.

Lift closes.

That's it, Eddie. That's what she meant. Of course I'm not ill. Look at me. I'm the picture of health. An accident. That's how it's going to happen. The question is . . . how?

SCENE FIVE – FLAT

Eddie is making a fry-up. He takes food from stove.

EDDIE Are you sure you don't want your sausages?

RICHIE No I do not. I'm not taking any chances.

EDDIE Okey dokey matey.

Throws the frying pan at Richie, who is hiding under the upturned sofa.

RICHIE What was that apocalyptic clonk?

EDDIE Well I didn't see anything. Relax old chum, I'm on guard, remember?

RICHIE I must be hallucinating – three days now with no food or water. Still I'm safe here under the sofa. I've only got to make it until the moon comes up tonight and then I'll have something to eat all right. There's a couple of 'Taiwanese Ranch-Style Jumbo Fish Burgers' in the freezer that have got my name on them.

EDDIE No, you've had them.

RICHIE No I haven't.

EDDIE Yeah, you had 'em for lunch remember.

RICHIE But I haven't had anything to eat for the last three days.

EDDIE Well no obviously you didn't eat them. I ate them for you. You made me test them for poison remember? Like I've been testing everything. Bloody knackered I am – you're lucky to have such a good mate. I tested all that Indian takeaway, those three pizzas, bottle of scotch – I had to test all that. Totally tested out the drinks cabinet. Things got so bad, I had to test that box of liqueur chocolates we'd been saving for our anniversary.

RICHIE I'm starving I am. Has the moon come up yet Eddie?

EDDIE I can't see from here.

RICHIE Well go and have a look.

EDDIE You go and have a look.

RICHIE I can't go near the window, you know that. Anything could happen. Suppose some Arab terrorist was on his way to blow up the Houses of Parliament, and he's sitting on top of the number nine bus, and he sees me at the window and mistakes me for President Bush on a fact finding mission. Kerblam! Or I might fall out. Or the window might fall in.

EDDIE Well I can't go, they might think I'm Sean Connery.

RICHIE What? You don't look a bit like Sean Connery.

EDDIE (*Doing an impression.*) Hello, my name's James Bond, not a lot of people know that.

Richie looks hard at Eddie and sighs.

RICHIE I don't know, maybe death'd be a blessed release.

EDDIE (*Continuing the impression.*) Zulus. Thousands of 'em. Wait till you see the whites of their eyes, lads. They would have won if they'd kept their eyes closed – not a lot of people know that.

RICHIE Eddie, Eddie, Eddie.

EDDIE What?

RICHIE Here's five pence. Shut up and go and see if the moon's come up.

EDDIE That's two things.

RICHIE So?

EDDIE Two things is ten pence.

RICHIE All right, here you are – swindler.

Eddie crosses to the window.

RICHIE Well, what does it look like?

EDDIE Well it's all so hard to tell. It's all so glum and cloudy. You know, like it normally is. Hard to tell whether it's day or night. Shall I switch the telly on and see if it's evening yet?

RICHIE Yes, go on old sport.

Eddie switches on the TV. We hear two bars of the Neighbours *theme tune.*

EDDIE Well, it could be any time really.

RICHIE Oh blast that vicious old gypsy slagwagon! I've been stuck underneath the sofa for three days now – absolutely nothing's happened. Well I'm fed up with it. I'm going to the lavvy once and for all. I'm not scared of any silly mumbo jumbo. If it's coming, it's coming. I'm not scared. I'm going to stare fate right in the face.

He walks straight onto the leading edge of the open door very heavily.

Oh God!

Staggers back to the sofa as quickly as he can.

It's true! It's true! Did you see that Eddie? You see, it could come from anywhere. Should the ceiling be sagging like that? What is it? What have you got up there?

EDDIE That's my piano.

RICHIE What, in the middle of the room?

EDDIE Yeah.

RICHIE Well, that's dangerous, that shouldn't be up there! Go up there and shift it.

EDDIE It'll cost you.

RICHIE All right. There's a twenty pee bit inside a polythene bag sellotaped to the bottom of the cistern.

EDDIE (*Leaving.*) Rightio.

RICHIE Hurry up.

EDDIE Running all the way.

Eddie saunters out of the living room.

RICHIE Oh Lord, you won't know me – but my name's Richard Richard, and you won't know me because I've led such a quiet and blameless life. Well, apart from that incident with the oven-ready chicken – but I have already apologised about that. I don't know if you remember, but I did. Anyway, the thing is . . . look, we haven't got much time . . . I was wondering if I could do a little deal with you. You see because I don't deserve any of this at all, but I know somebody who does. Eddie, that chap who just went out. (*We hear a few notes being played on the piano.*) Because he's a foul pervert and a dole scrounger. (*To Eddie.*) Look just stop piddling around and move it will you, you bastard? (*To God.*) No no, not you sir, our Lord, I was talking to Eddie – the evil one. The thing is, if you could see your way clear to murdering him horribly instead of me, then I promise, and I mean it – look I haven't got my fingers crossed or anything – I promise that I'll go to church for the rest of my life. You do still do that thing with the wine and biscuits don't you? Great. Thank you for your time. Oooh one other thing, Lord. If you're still there. Seeing as I'm going to live, it's about girls. I was . . . (*More piano noises.*) Shut up Eddie! . . . I was wondering if I could just have a few more . . .

Will you shut up Eddie? . . . Well just one, once I mean . . . right! That's it!

He runs to the door.

RICHIE Edward Hitler, come down here at once.

Eddie crashes through the ceiling with the piano. Right onto the spot Richie just vacated.

RICHIE It's you!

EDDIE Well who'd you expect it to be?

RICHIE You're the one! You're the one who said, 'Let's go to the fair'. You're the one who shot the thug in the eye. You're the one who said, 'Let's hide in the gypsy's tent' where I got the curse. And then on the third night just before the moon rises, you drop a piano on my head! You bastard! You're after Auntie Olga's three hundred quid aren't you? Well, I've got news for you buster.

Picks up the poker and starts hitting Eddie with it. Clang! Clang! Eddie's only partially conscious anyway.

You're out of here. (*Thwack. Thwack.*) You're history. (*Clang, Chirrup.*) How could you treat a friend so badly? I'd never do anything like that.

Smashes the poker so hard that it curls round Eddie's head.

Go on, get out of here before I set the dogs on you.

EDDIE We haven't got any dogs.

RICHIE Yes I know we haven't! (*Hit.*) It was (*Hit*) a (*Hit*) figure (*Hit*) of (*Hit*) speech. Get out!

He pushes Eddie out of the door and down the stairs.

RICHIE And good riddance!

Richie looks at the mangled poker.

RICHIE My poker!

SCENE SIX – RICHIE'S BEDROOM

RICHIE Ha ha ha. Safe at last. Well I think I'll just pop into bed with my hotty botty.

Gets into bed.

RICHIE Where's my bedside book? Ah, here we are – *War and Peace*. We've been at it a few years now haven't we old mate? Where was I?

He's flicking through the whole book. Gets to near the beginning.

Ah yes. Chapter One, sentence three.

He reads.

Here we go again. Where's the dictionary? I'll never find out who did it at this rate. I'll be lucky enough to find out what it was they did! Oh that's enough reading for one night. Good for the soul though, a bit of reading. No doubt about that. Ooh I'm all relaxed now. That's nice. D'you know I think I might . . . no, I'll just go to sleep. Nightie-night world. God bless me. See you in the morning – not too early. Ah well, heigh ho.

He settles down then there is a creaking noise.

RICHIE No, no. Ah!

There is more creaking.

RICHIE Oh it's bloody Eddie. It's bloody Eddie sneaking in to get me as soon as I switch the lights out. I've got a surprise for him. Where's my cricket bat?

Richie finds his cricket bat and goes to his door. He stands poised to hit Eddie with it. There is a tapping at the door.

RICHIE Come in.

The door opens. There is horror on Richie's face. At the door is the figure of Death. Eight feet tall in a black cowl and carrying a scythe. Richie falls back in terror. Death strides spookily into the room.

RICHIE Are you . . . are you . . .?

Death nods.

RICHIE And have you come for . . .?

Death nods again. Richie gasps. He stumbles back into the curtains pulling them down. Moonlight floods into room.

RICHIE No, no. Oh my God the moon's up! Oh my God. She was right! She was right! Oh my God! Jesus H. Corbett . . . I mean Christ! This can't be happening to me. No. Come on, come on, let's be English about this. Excuse me, this is a private house, if you don't clear off my property immediately, I shall be forced to call the police!

Death rips the phone out of the wall and flings it through the window.

RICHIE OK, point taken. So, this is it is it?

Death nods.

RICHIE I haven't got time, I'm not ready! Have I got time to change? I can't really go up there in my jimmy jams can I? What would Saint Pete think? They do call him Saint Pete don't they? First impressions are terribly important I always feel. Unless . . . Which way am I going, up or . . .?

Death starts to point upwards then plunges his finger down like a Roman emperor. Richie gasps.

RICHIE Aaagh!

Richie collapses into hacking sobs on the bed.

Death takes a step towards him, beckoning. But then loses his balance. He totters and has to trot the length of the room and balance himself against the wall. It is almost as if he was on stilts. He pushes himself up from the wall and totters dangerously back towards the door, then out of the door into the corridor, coming to a stop against the wall.

Richie is face down sobbing into the pillow, he notices none of this.

Trying to get upright, Death swings his scythe about wildly. As he stumbles back into the room, the hood of his cowl gets caught in the door jam and is pulled off revealing Eddie underneath. He flaps about wildly trying to get his hood back on, and only just manages it before Richie lifts his head from the pillow. Death is panting as Richie says:

RICHIE Wait! Wait! What about chess?

EDDIE (*In a disguised 'death' voice.*) What about it?

RICHIE Why don't we play a game of chess?

EDDIE Because I don't know the rules.

RICHIE Well that's all right, I can teach you the rules.

EDDIE No. You won't need rules where you're going mate – you'll need asbestos underpants. 'Cos you're going downstairs me old cocker. Ooh the moans, ooh the screams, the countless billions thrown naked into the pit . . . .

RICHIE Naked? Hmmmn. Wait. What about Cluedo?

EDDIE No, they tried it once mate, but all the pieces caught fire.

RICHIE No, I mean, why don't we play Cluedo for my life?

EDDIE Because you always cheat – you always look at the mystery cards.

RICHIE (*Gasps.*) How do you know these things?

EDDIE I'm Death.

RICHIE (*Shouting.*) Sorry! I said, 'How do you know these things?'!!!

EDDIE No, I'm *Death*! I'm *Death*!!!

RICHIE Oh if only Eddie were here.

EDDIE Yeah, Eddie was pretty great at everything, wasn't he?

RICHIE Well you wouldn't have come in if he was here mate – the pong would have sent you round the twist.

EDDIE Right, that's it mate. Your time's up, time to get a red hot trident up your jacksy.

RICHIE No, no please give me one more chance. I-Spy?

EDDIE Mmmmn! . . . OK.

RICHIE OK. And if I win I get to live, OK?

EDDIE Okey dokey matey.

RICHIE Pardon?

EDDIE I mean all right mortal.

RICHIE (*Looking quizzical for a moment.*) No, it's not possible. OK. I-Spy it is. Oh God this is important. I'd better make it a goody. OK coming, ready or not. I spy, with my little eye, something beginning with 's'.

EDDIE Submarine.

RICHIE No.

EDDIE What do you mean? It begins with an 's'.

RICHIE Yeah, but you can't see one can you?

Pause.

EDDIE I see everything.

RICHIE Yeah, but it's got to be something we can both see.

EDDIE Oh I see, changing the rules now are you?

RICHIE Oh don't be ridiculous you big tit.

EDDIE (*Menacingly.*) Careful mortal!

RICHIE (*Scared.*) Oh sorry. Go on, have another go, 's'.

Eddie totters around the room looking for something beginning with 'S'.

EDDIE Ha ha! Got it . . . Selina Scott!!

RICHIE No. It was 'scythe'! Aha! I win! I get to live! Thank you baby Jesus, thank you all the baby Jesuses.

EDDIE Hang on, hang on – 'scythe' doesn't begin with an 's'.

RICHIE Yes it does.

EDDIE Bloody doesn't, it's a 'c'

RICHIE It is not.

EDDIE It is. Get a dictionary.

RICHIE All right, I've got one here. Here! Scythe . . . scythe . . . scythe . . . there you are scythe – S.C.Y.T.H.E.

EDDIE That's zither.

RICHIE It's scythe. It says scythe there. It's in the dictionary. Jesus wrote that.

EDDIE All right then mortal, I can see you're eager to keep your life. How's about I offer you a straight deal?

RICHIE A deal? Sure, no problem, great.

Death draws himself up to his full height and leans on the open door.

EDDIE How much money have you got in the house?

RICHIE None.

EDDIE What about the three hundred quid on top of the bathroom cabinet?

RICHIE How do you know about that?

EDDIE God I keep telling you mate, I'm Death, I know everything.

RICHIE Everything? What – even about the . . . .

EDDIE Especially that, you naughty boy.

RICHIE OK. I'll get the money. Just don't tell anybody. You wait right here.

He nips out. Death falls over as Richie slams the door. He has great trouble getting back onto his stilts before Richie re-enters with £300 in his hand.

RICHIE Here we are, so I give you the three hundred pounds and I get to keep my life, OK?

EDDIE Not quite, no. The full deal is this. I get to keep the three hundred pounds and your fantastic mate Eddie gets to live here rent-free for the rest of his life.

RICHIE OK, it's a deal.

EDDIE And while I'm at it, I'll have that secret copy of *Girlie World* you keep under your mattress.

Richie weighs it up for a moment.

EDDIE Or you'll burn in the fires of Hell.

RICHIE All right.

He retrieves the magazine from under his mattress and gives it to Eddie.

EDDIE Bye.

RICHIE Is that everything now?

EDDIE That's it mate, cheerio!

He rushes out.

EDDIE Ha ha! Three hundred quid and a copy of *Girlie World*. Ha ha ha. Ooh blimey!

He falls headlong down the stairs, tumble tumble. He ends up in a heap at the bottom of the stairs. His costume has fallen off revealing a broken pair of broom handles tied to his legs. Richie rushes to the stair head and sees everything.

EDDIE Oooh blimey, I think I've broken me stilts!

RICHIE Edward Hitler! You total bastard! How did you know about my secret copy of *Girlie World*? Right, that's it. You're going to get a knuckle sandwich, and I don't mean a sandwich with some knuckles in it, well I do actually, well no I don't really but, well, you're going to get a smash in the chops and no questions answered anyway.

He rushes downstairs. He is stopped in his tracks by the sound of heavy beating on the front door below.

RICHIE Well who on earth can that be at this time of night?

We hear the sound of the door being smashed off its hinges and someone coming up the stairs.

EDDIE Well, I'm not expecting anyone.

RICHIE Maybe it's the real Death!

EDDIE Hey now that'd be a turn up.

Crash.

RICHIE Ooooh blimey, blimey, Eddie you fight him to the death and I'll slip down the fire escape.

EDDIE Too late.

He points to the man from the shooting gallery who is at the top of the stairs. He has a bandage over his right eye.

MAN Sir Richard Richard, Esq?

RICHIE & EDDIE (*Pointing at each other.*) That's him.

MAN I've got your wallet.

BOTH Oh that'll be me, then.

RICHIE How very honest of you. D'you know, I have always said that you Romany types were as generous as the day is . . . .

MAN Well the credit cards have expired and the driving licence is a forgery, and apart from the nudey collage of Julia Somerville, it's of no use to me – rather like my eye.

RICHIE So that's how she knew all those things!

Eddie reacts.

MAN Now, how much money have you got in the house?

RICHIE None.

MAN Well what about that three hundred pounds I've heard about that you've got safely ensconced on top of the bathroom cabinet.

EDDIE (*Trying to hide the money.*) Em . . . it . . . it . . . it's not there anymore.

MAN Well I'll just have to have this then.

He swipes the £300 from Eddie.

MAN That should just about cover the three hundred pounds they told me in Harley Street it would cost to get my eye fixed. Yeah, while I'm here, I think I'll have that copy of *Girlie World* an' all.

He snatches it from Eddie.

RICHIE A very wise choice sir. Oh, one more thing.

MAN Yeah?

RICHIE Well seeing as you're here, would you like to kick Eddie in the bollocks?

MAN Don't mind if I do, thank you very much.

RICHIE Be my guest.

The man kicks Eddie.

Fin.

BOTTOMS UP

SCENE ONE – FLAT

Richie is cleaning up

RICHIE (*Sings.*) Land of Hope and Glory . . . something, something else. Land of Hope and Glo . . . Glo . . . Glory. That is where I live. Land of Hope and Glory.

Drops rubbish out of the window.

Morning! Oh! What a lovely day. God I love Sundays. Sunday papers, stroll in the park, church, and back home for a nice big joint of good old English beef. Strawberries and cream, a spot of tennis, and a smile in the heart of every true Englishman. (*To someone outside below*) Morning Vicar, lovely day! (*Inaudible reply.*) Charming! Somebody got out of bed the wrong side this morning. Mind you, he got out of the womb the wrong side. (*Shouting down.*) And the same to you with brass knobs on, you steaming great twat! Oh, I do feel great today. Oh, the English summertime. Gets you right there doesn't it Eddie? Eddie? Eddie, have you ever seen such glorious sunshine?

EDDIE Close the curtains, I'm trying to watch the TV.

RICHIE Oh Eddie don't be like that, we should be out there playing cricket. Come on, it's Sunday, it's a day of rest. Absolutely nothing to do for twenty-four hours.

EDDIE That's a bit like every other day then really isn't it?

RICHIE Oh come on Eddie. We can't sit around watching videos all day. It's a lovely day, the bluebirds are singing . . .

EDDIE Look! Close the curtains! It's just about to get to the exciting bit. (*Pause*.) Now!

RICHIE OK! Right! Right! OK!

Richie closes the curtains in a kind of sulk. They are lost in the gloom.

RICHIE Well, this is great isn't it?

EDDIE Yes, it's just dandy.

RICHIE I cooked you a breakfast you know.

Pause

Can't find it now. Have to get the torch out.

Gets torch

Breakfast! Where are you? Breakfast!

EDDIE What is it?

RICHIE It's your favourite Eddie. I cooked you your . . . da da da da da da da . . . Sunday fishfinger.

EDDIE But I don't like fishfingers.

RICHIE Oh no of course, you don't do you? I make that mistake every Sunday don't I? Oh well never mind. (*Eddie mimes along with this last bit.*) I'll eat yours for you. Mmmm mmmm mmmm.

Richie's face turns to one of disgust and he spits out the fishfinger.

RICHIE Who's that anyway?

EDDIE Oh that's mother bear.

RICHIE I thought she was dead?

EDDIE No no, that's Mr Rabbit. Anyway he's not dead, he's just asleep in the dingly dell. That's how he missed his birthday tea and why they're all out looking for him.

Pause

RICHIE It's not very sexy is it?

EDDIE No. I must say I expected a lot more from *The Furry Honeypot Adventure*.

RICHIE I think this is for kids you know, Eddie. I think those Hussein brothers saw you coming again. What else did you get?

EDDIE *Big Jugs*.

RICHIE *Big Jugs*? All right . . .

Richie opens the case and examines the contents. He reads.

RICHIE *A History of Pottery in the Nineteenth Century*. Anything else?

EDDIE Well, this one's a sure fire hit – *Swedish Lesbians in Blackcurrant Jam*.

RICHIE Yabadabadoo!!

Richie reads it

No Eddie, it's *Swedish Legends in Blackcurrant Jam-making*.

EDDIE Oh come on, it's got to be dirty – it says Swedish! Oh what a disaster! That's my whole Sunday ruined! I spent an hour choosing them. What a swizz! Ah well, maybe we should stick with *The Furry Honeypot Adventure*, you never know it might perk up in a minute.

Pause. They check the video for dirt.

RICHIE Hey up! Look here comes that rabbit again.

EDDIE Well, now he's up we should be on for a bit of action.

RICHIE Yeah, I mean he's a rabbit for Christ's sake.

EDDIE Yeah. Right here he goes . . . into the house . . . and there's Mrs Bear . . . Heeeh . . . go on my son . . . he's creeping up behind her . . . he's going to surprise her . . . and here come all the baby bears . . . and they're all singing happy birthday . . . and having a bit of a dance . . . Tchhh . . . it's not going to get very dirty is it?

RICHIE No. You can sort of tell that can't you, by the way it says, 'The End'.

EDDIE Yeah. Well I'm bloody sick, I don't mind telling you.

Richie opens the curtains

RICHIE Well I'm rather glad they weren't dirty actually. I don't think as a Christian I could look myself in the face whilst watching a dirty video. I mean it's Sunday for Christ's sake, I mean for Heaven's . . . I mean for Goodness' sake. And are the masses all in church praising the Lord's name? No. They're all down the vid shop trying to get hold of *Pervy Nights in Bangkok*. I mean, it's ironic isn't it – there's plenty of wailing and gnashing of teeth going on, but it's not happening in church.

EDDIE Well when did you last go to church?

RICHIE Well I don't have to go, I'm Church of England.

Eddie reacts

RICHIE What are you Eddie?

EDDIE I don't know.

RICHIE Well what was your mother?

EDDIE A wrestler.

RICHIE Well, maybe that's enough general knowledge for one day.

There is tapping at the door

BOTH Go away!

Mr Harrison bursts in. Mr Harrison is always in a bad mood.

HARRISON Hello gentlemen.

RICHIE Ooh. Er, Mr Harrison! Hello! Look, sorry about the rent, the fact is the Kruggerand's just crashed so we had to move into junk bonds and we couldn't get them out of Lichtenstein till the end of the month. (*Ushering him out.*) I knew you'd understand.

Closes the door on him.

That was a close one.

Tap tap tap.

Come in!

Harrison comes back in

Oh this is intolerable – talk about Rachman.

HARRISON Look I'm not here for the rent . . .

RICHIE Oh great! Come in, sit down. Eddie – a cup of tea.

EDDIE Oh yes please.

HARRISON Look boys, you've got to help me – I'm in a dreadful fix. I completely forgot about my stupid mother's bloody funeral.

RICHIE Oh! Is she dead?

HARRISON Well let's hope so – bloody coffin cost me two hundred quid. Cow! Anyway, I got to go. Please can you run the shop for me?

RICHIE I'm sorry Mr Harrison, but I have to confess to being frankly really rather shocked. I mean me? Run a shop? On a Sunday of all things? Absolutely not!

HARRISON Fifty quid.

RICHIE You're on!

EDDIE When do we start?

HARRISON Right away, I've got to be in Penge by noon, come on . . . (*Exiting.*) I'll show you the ropes.

RICHIE (*Exiting.*) Ah no, no. I'm sorry I don't do lifting, you'll have to show Eddie the ropes – show me the till.

EDDIE No no no no. Show me the drinks section and the sign that says 'closed'.

SCENE TWO – SHOP

Harrison, Richie and Eddie come into the shop through the door marked, 'This is not a toilet'.

HARRISON Why can't they just stick them in a bin? All this palaver.

RICHIE Mr Harrison! Have you got a sort of white coat or something? So that everyone knows that I'm the shopkeeper?

HARRISON Yes, hang on I'll get you one.

He scurries about sorting out Richie's coat.

HARRISON Here you are. And here's one for you Eddie.

Richie pulls it away

RICHIE Well no, no, no, no, haven't you got a sort of brown one for him?

HARRISON No. Of course I haven't.

RICHIE What about a little badge or something that just says 'assistant'?

Harrison shakes his head.

HARRISON What are you talking about? Look I'm in a hurry.

RICHIE All right, all right well look Eddie, you'll just have to put your jacket on back to front or something.

EDDIE Piss off!

RICHIE Oh don't kick up a stink Eddie, I know what I'm doing. It's nothing personal, it's just that there is a sort of upstairs downstairs thing to any shopping experience which the shopper needs to feel reassured about.

EDDIE (*Grudgingly.*) All right.

He puts his jacket on back to front.

RICHIE There. Now everybody knows who everybody is.

HARRISON (*Sarky.*) Everybody happy now?

RICHIE Yes, thank you.

HARRISON Right, there's thirty pounds in change in the till, if you'd just sign there. I'd better be off. See you later. Two hundred pounds for a coffin and they set fire to the bastard.

Harrison leaves in a hurry. The boys reflect on their sudden change of circumstances.

RICHIE Well this is a bit of all right isn't it Eddie?

EDDIE Yeah, shame he hasn't got a video section.

Eddie helps himself to cans of lager and crisps and settles down to read the papers.

RICHIE It's a very dignified thing being a shopkeeper don't you think? You know, there's power, integrity, snazzy coat.

Goes into a reverie. He strides about a bit.

Yeah, yeah. Morning, morning. Morning your lordship. Oh yes, plenty of gravy-mix. You help yourself – I'll just put it on the slate.

Turns to another, smaller, imaginary customer

Oy, what do you think you're doing?

Mimes twisting a small kid's ear.

Shoplifting eh sonny? (*Pokes him.*) Eh? Eh? Eh? (*Pokes him harder and harder, pushing him across the shop.*) What's the matter, haven't you got enough money? So you thought you'd take it out on me just because I *work so hard*? (*Mimes pulling the boy's head off.*) Spurt spurt spurt! (*Mimes putting it back on again.*) Only kidding, little kiddie. Go on, take your Jaffa Cakes and run along. Go on. Off you go. Oh God why did you make me so nice?

The imaginary boy leaves

Has he gone? Right.

Richie produces an imaginary phone

Beep beep boo beep! Hello Police, I want to report a theft. Yeah it was little Johnny Cartwright from the flats. Nail the sucker, bust his ass. Yeah, I want him doing twenty to ten in the pen . . . what do you mean no evidence?! What about the goddam Jaffa Cakes, asswipe? Yeah? Bull*shit*! Bull*shit*! Yeah? Well I'm going to get Mayor Dooley to . . .

A little old lady comes in behind him and takes him by surprise. They look at each other in surprise. Pause.

LADY What's the matter, are you mad?

Richie is furious, and embarrassed. He starts pushing his fist at her face.

RICHIE Do you want some of this? Do you? Cause you're going to get it you old git! You're going to get a right load of this right up your bracket! Right in your face.

The old lady turns and goes out.

That's right, run! Go on! Just like you did at Goose Green! Argie!

He calms down a bit.

(*To an unseen person.*) Morning! See, British shopkeeping, Eddie – best in the world. Yes. Yes.

He walks back towards the counter. He picks up a tin.

Tuna. Good. We're a nation of shopkeepers you know. Oh yeah, that's what makes us so great you know. They don't call it Great Luxembourg do they? No. Or Great France?

EDDIE What's so great about being a nation of shopkeepers?

RICHIE What's so great about being a nation of shopkeepers?!

EDDIE Yeah, what's so great about it?

RICHIE Well, it makes us superior to everyone else, because we know how to run a corner shop. Good grief Eddie, it only takes an ounce of brain power to see that.

EDDIE Well that should suit you perfectly then.

RICHIE How do you mean? I don't understand that.

Eddie looks up from his paper

EDDIE Cor . . . The whole cast of *Brookside* are lesbians.

RICHIE Yeah. British journalism, Eddie – best in the world.

EDDIE Bloody Nora! Neil Kinnock's grandparents were homosexual Martians! He's kept quiet about that hasn't he? Lucky I read that – I was going to vote Labour.

RICHIE Yeah, another great British scoop Eddie. I'd like to see the *Amsterdam Evening News* dig up something like that. Frogs.

EDDIE Hell's teeth! You can get AIDS from bicycling?

RICHIE I know, I know. And isn't it funny that you only read that sort of thing in a British newspaper?

EDDIE Yeah well you don't read French or Italian papers do you?

RICHIE Well I don't speak French or Italian. Good grief Eddie. Hold together a cogent argument, why don't you?

He reads

Oh here we go, holidays in the Algarve! Look at this, no electricity, no running water, and fifteen hundred quid a month. People pay for this. South of France?! We bloody invented it mate! George the Third, he was the one, all that swimming business. And the windbreak? Who invented that? We did! The Brits! Never mind covering yourself in Mazola and lying around with a bit of string up your crack. No. A quick dip in the briny, dig up a lugworm, and back in the car before you get pneumonia. Yup, that's good enough for me. Ooh! Look at this! Thirty-eight quid return coach trip to Nice. 'Nude beach'.

A man (Mr Cooper) comes in to the shop and comes up to the counter.

MR COOPER Excuse me, I didn't get my paper this morning.

RICHIE So? It's not my problem. You should be more careful.

MR COOPER No, it wasn't delivered.

RICHIE Oh, I get it. Trying to get a free paper are we? Spend all morning doing that and you could open up a little paper shop couldn't you?

MR COOPER Look, I don't know what your game is, but I didn't get my paper delivered this morning. Now I have *The Mail on Sunday*, so if I could just take one now please?

EDDIE But that's the last copy.

MR COOPER Okay I'll take that one.

RICHIE Hang on, hang on, I'm reading that.

MR COOPER Yeah but it's mine. (*Notices writing on the paper*) Look, it's even got my name on it.

RICHIE That's your name is it? Fifty-five pee, Mr Fifty-five pee.

MR COOPER No, my name is Cooper – look it's written in biro in the corner.

Richie looks then rips the name off the corner of paper.

RICHIE All right then Mr Cooper. There's your paper. Good morning.

MR COOPER Where's the rest of it?

RICHIE What do you mean, 'Where's the rest of it?'

MR COOPER I would like the rest of my paper.

RICHIE Well then, I suggest you go outside, knock and come in and ask for it nicely.

MR COOPER Right!

Mr Cooper slams Richie's head onto the counter and takes the paper.

MR COOPER See you, Eddie.

EDDIE Yeah bye, John.

RICHIE . . . Thug.

EDDIE British thugs, Richie – best in the world.

RICHIE Damn, we should have written down the particulars of that nudey beach trip.

EDDIE Well there is a nudey beach in Brighton, you know. It's twelve pound, sixty-nine pence exactly on the Intercity Saver and the nipples are bigger – it's the cold wind. They've got these telescopes that you put twenty pence in. It's very discreet.

RICHIE Oh! Let's go! No, no no no! We've got to run the shop. That's what makes us British you see Eddie. Your average Frog or Brussel Sprout'd be half way down the A3 by now, polishing up his zoom lens and sticking bits of garlic up his bum. Not us.

EDDIE Well not you maybe . . .

Eddie makes to go.

RICHIE Eddie! Stand firm! Where were you at Agincourt?

EDDIE I stayed on the bus remember? With Ethel Cardew.

RICHIE No no shut up, I wasn't talking about that.

EDDIE Oh that's why you don't like France.

RICHIE I don't want to hear this.

EDDIE You don't like France 'cause you've only ever had one bird, and I shagged her on a Christmas Club coach trip to Bruges.

Pause.

RICHIE Eddie, she was my fiancée.

EDDIE Well she didn't know that.

RICHIE Well I hadn't told her yet had I? I was going to propose to her. But I wanted to make it romantic. That's why I decided to take her on a cultural tour of the battlefields of the Low Countries.

EDDIE But I decided to come along, didn't I?

RICHIE Yes.

EDDIE I showed her the Low Countries all right, I showed her the nether regions.

RICHIE All right, all right.

EDDIE They came at Bruges, they came at Agincourt . . . Talk about the battle of the bulge!

RICHIE Well I blame myself for being car sick all over her.

Ting! Another man comes into the shop

EDDIE Blimey, it's all go today isn't it?

RICHIE And a very good morning to you sir, and how may I be of assistance to you on this merry day?

DOCTOR (*Good humouredly joining in the banter.*) And good morning to you. Now, 'assistant', what I'd like this fine morning . . .

RICHIE Excuse, hang on, hang on j j j j j! Let's just get one thing clear shall we? I am not an assistant – I am a shopkeeper.

DOCTOR Is there a difference?

RICHIE Is there a difference? I've got a white coat on and he's got his jacket on back to front – and that's just the tip of the iceberg mate. So let's show a bit of respect shall we? What would you like?

DOCTOR (*Carefully.*) Er, that champagne please.

RICHIE Are you eighteen?

DOCTOR No, I'm fifty-four.

RICHIE So you're not eighteen then?

DOCTOR (*He snaps.*) Look, just get up the ladder.

RICHIE Don't you take that kind of tone with me young lad, you've got to be eighteen if you want to buy alcohol. Look, it says it there.

DOCTOR 'Or over,' it says.

Pause.

RICHIE Eddie, get up the ladder.

EDDIE It's my lunch break.

Richie slaps Eddie about the head.

EDDIE All right, all right, I'm going.

Richie and the Doctor eyeball each other. Eddie goes up and brings a bottle down.

DOCTOR I want three bottles.

EDDIE What, are you an alcoholic?

DOCTOR It's my daughter's birthday.

RICHIE Ooh, it's his daughter's birthday so he's going to drink three bottles of champagne. Well there's modern parenthood for you.

As Eddie gets the other two bottles, the man gets something out of his pocket.

RICHIE What do you think you're doing with that?

DOCTOR This is a cheque book.

RICHIE But this card only guarantees you for fifty pounds. And I'm afraid these items cost more than fifty pounds. So I'm terribly sorry, you're going to have to . . .

Eddie clocks the problem. He 'tings' the till, the drawer shoots out and hits Richie in the goolies. Richie howls in pain and collapses beneath the counter.

EDDIE A cheque'll do nicely – just make it out to Eddie Hitler.

DOCTOR (*Writes.*) Hitler? Any relation?

EDDIE (*Proudly.*) Yes.

Doctor reacts.

Richie pulls himself up on the counter and grabs the cheque. He cross-references the signature with the one on the cheque card.

RICHIE So this is you, is it? This sort of squiggle is you? What do you do for a living? You some sort of modern artist are you?

DOCTOR I am a doctor. Now bugger off.

RICHIE Oh that's witty, isn't it? Took you five years at medical school to learn that one did it? – On my money, let's not forget that. Bloody students. You're all the same. I don't know why you don't just go and live in Russia.

The doctor leaves and Richie follows him.

Go on. Get out of my shop. Go on. Bugger off out of it. Go on. On your bicycle. Good grief Eddie, sometimes I think there's only you and me left. Eddie? . . . Eddie? Eddie? . . . Eddie? Eddie?

SCENE THREE – HALLWAY OUTSIDE RICHIE'S BEDROOM/ BEHIND LIVING ROOM

Eddie is revealed putting on his summer hat and other summery sort of things. Richie pants into view.

RICHIE Eddie? Eddie? What do you think you're doing?

EDDIE I am going to watch some cricket.

He opens a cupboard and starts throwing things up through the trap door on to the roof – deck chair, umbrella, tripod, telescope.

RICHIE You can't do that – what about the shop?

EDDIE I've had it with that shop-assisting lark. I resign.

RICHIE Well you won't get your share of the money you know.

Eddie and Richie walk into the shop from the hallway.

EDDIE (*Waving the doctor's cheque.*) Well I'm all right mate, I've already got a cheque for fifty-three quid.

RICHIE You bastard.

EDDIE Yeah, that's me.

RICHIE You're not going to get away with this you . . . miner! This is Britain. Do you hear me? Britain! You're not allowed to go on strike anymore, it's illegal and don't forget I'm a mason. Yeah! I've only got to drop the nod to Scotland Yard and this place will be full of armoured horses and tear gas before you can say, 'vote Labour'. What are you doing Eddie?

EDDIE Don't you worry, Richie, you're going to watch the cricket too.

RICHIE I am not – I've got social responsibilities. See this little old lady – we shall not fail her. See her walking. See her enormous son walking next to her. She looks like the one I threatened earlier. See his mighty tattoos. I think he's going to whack me.

The old lady and her beefy thug of a son's point of view.

OLD LADY (*Out of view.*) That's the one!

The son thwacks Richie on the nose.

EDDIE You were right.

RICHIE (*Checking for blood.*) Maybe watching the cricket would be a bit safer Eddie. What's the plan?

EDDIE Well, we sit up on the roof watching the cricket and having a bit of a picnic, someone comes into the shop, they open the door, the bell rings, we come down and serve them.

RICHIE Sounds smashing. Come on, let's get out of here.

EDDIE Rightio young sonny-jim old fellow-me-lad matey skip me old pal from the briny, let's fill up the picnic hamper.

Eddie scoops armfuls of provisons off the shelves into his basket.

SCENE FOUR – ROOF

Richie and Eddie are ensconced on the roof. They have a large feast before them and are watching the cricket through binoculars and telescope. The game is obviously several miles away.

EDDIE Here he comes . . . here he comes . . . and he's out! No no, hang on – he's back in again. Oh, she's closed the curtains. How's the cricket going?

RICHIE Well it still hasn't started yet. (*Looking through his telescope.*) These stumps are very big aren't they?

EDDIE Let's have a look. (*Looks.*) That's the rugby ground. The cricket's over there. What's going on?

RICHIE They've broken for lunch.

EDDIE Why are you putting mayonnaise on your face?

RICHIE It's not mayonnaise – it's sun-tan lotion.

EDDIE I've never heard of low calorie sun-tan lotion before.

RICHIE What! (*Looks.*) Oh no! Blast! Oh God. Oh look, well where's the sun-tan lotion then?

EDDIE You squirted that into your cheese roll.

RICHIE But I ate that?!

EDDIE Yeah I know.

RICHIE Well why didn't you tell me?

EDDIE Because I don't like you very much.

Pause.

RICHIE Now I know you're joking me.

RICHIE Ah! This is the life, isn't it?

Aeroplane sound effects.

I should have been a farmer you know. I really am an earth child. I know the deep movement.

EDDIE Only deep movement you know is when you've had a curry.

RICHIE I'm part Red Indian you know.

EDDIE That'll be the curry again.

RICHIE No, I am Cherokee. D'you know I can even tell when it's going to rain.

EDDIE How do you do that?

RICHIE Well I sort of look up mystically, you know, check out the sky, if I see any black clouds, that's it, I think, rain.

EDDIE What was your Red Indian name then? Running Mouth? Sitting Down? Talking Bollocks?

RICHIE Dances with the Wind.

EDDIE That'll be the curry again.

RICHIE Well, I'd advise you to take me seriously young man or I might very well make it rain.

EDDIE Oh that'll be good. Go on then breezy trousers or whatever your name is, make it rain.

RICHIE Eddie, you don't dabble with the deep forces.

EDDIE (*Looking up.*) Look, there's not a cloud in the sky. I'll give you twenty-five quid if you can make it rain.

RICHIE You're on. Right, I shall need a tomahawk. Oh this'll do. (*Picks up fly swat.*) No it's good actually. Right. Now this may not work properly Eddie – I'm used to working in moccasins. Right, put up your brolly this is going to be a big one. (*Richie begins chant and dance and strains his groin.*) Ooh! Jesus oh! (*Chants again.*) Hoom alla pappyon oom alla pappyon om alla pappyon oom pah . . . Rain!

A seagull poos on Richie's head

It worked – look Eddie. Urgh! Bloody hell. Oh God! I must have used the wrong chant.

EDDIE What are you going to do now then? Bring down a typhoon of buffalo dung?

RICHIE I'd advise you to take me seriously mate, or I'll invoke the Big Spirit – and he doesn't mess around.

EDDIE Oh pull the other one mate it's got bells on.

We hear the sound of the bell from below.

EDDIE (*Worried.*) How'd you do that?

RICHIE Mystical forces Eddie, mystical forces.

EDDIE Rubbish. It's the shop – we've got a customer.

Eddie climbs through the trap door.

RICHIE Eddie, careful with that step.

EDDIE What step? Aargh!

Crash.

Richie rigs Eddie's chair to collapse. Goes to the hatch to shout down to him.

Eddie I've got a lovely chair for you! Eddie! Maybe he's not coming up.

Pulls at the hatch. It won't open. Worries. Tugs at it.

Eddie, Eddie, I'm stuck on the roof, Eddie. I'm trapped – you can't open it from out here. Eddie!!! Mayday! Mayday!

The trap door swings up violently into his face. Eddie appears. He can't see Richie behind the trap.

EDDIE You OK Richie?

RICHIE I think I've broken my nose.

EDDIE Oh well come on, you'd better have sit down then.

RICHIE Thanks mate.

He helps Richie to a chair. It is the collapsible chair. It collapses. Richie writhes in agony.

RICHIE Oh me back.

EDDIE Well you're lucky mate – you should see what's just happened downstairs.

RICHIE Why, who was it?

EDDIE Well, that's the strange thing, there was no one there. Just this bloke lying in the doorway with a bell in the back of his head.

RICHIE Did you put the bell back up?

EDDIE Certainly did mate.

Klang ow! Someone below gets it

EDDIE Another customer. Your turn.

RICHIE Oh be an angel, Eddie. I've smashed my face in and broken my back, I don't think I could handle three flights.

EDDIE Three quid.

RICHIE Two pound fifty.

EDDIE Six quid.

RICHIE You're on. You're on. Doesn't do to haggle with Eddie too long. Eddie, be careful with that step!

EDDIE Right! Argh!

Crash.

Richie recovers and sets about fixing the trap door to fall on Eddie's head when he comes back up. He removes the string that is partially holding up the guttering, and ties it to the stick holding the trap door up.

RICHIE Tie the string here. Ooh! Careful, careful. Right, I need some bait. What does Eddie like best? A pickled onion sandwich. Right.

He picks up the bread and onion. He puts the onion in the bread. He puts the sandwich just by the trap door.

RICHIE Perfect. Eddie! Oh Eddie! I've made your favourite – a pickled onion sandwich!

Richie moves to chimneys

Right. I hide here. Eddie comes up. Sees the sandwich. Says 'Ooh, a pickled onion sandwich – my favourite.' I pull the string. Cricket bat comes out. Whack – Eddie gets full force of the trap door in the back of the head. Nothing can go wrong.

Eddie appears silently and climbs out. Looks about for Richie. Sees sandwich. Picks it up and goes to seat.

EDDIE Oh great, a pickled onion sandwich – my favourite.

RICHIE Right get a load of this you bastard.

Richie pulls the string and the trap door closes.

RICHIE Ha ha got you!

He sees Eddie in seat and notices the trap door is shut fast.

RICHIE Eddie you stupid idiot. You let the trap door shut. We're stuck on the roof now.

EDDIE Well how's that my fault?

RICHIE Well you were supposed to stop it with your head.

EDDIE Well I didn't know anything about this.

RICHIE Well of course you didn't, it was a surprise – it was a joke.

EDDIE But that would have hurt wouldn't it?

RICHIE Exactly! That's what was so funny about it.

Eddie thinks for a moment then goes to Richie. He is about to punch him.

RICHIE Don't you dare.

The bell clangs.

EDDIE Another customer.

RICHIE But we're stuck on the roof Eddie!

EDDIE Well what about the fire escape?

RICHIE No good, it collapsed remember when 'Tubbs' Lardy won that bet that it wouldn't hold his weight.

EDDIE Yeah I remember. Shocking mess. That dustbin's still flat.

RICHIE I know. And the cat's still in it. You can hear it when you shake it about.

EDDIE Well what are we going to do about this customer?

RICHIE Well perhaps you should shout down and tell him that some bald-headed loony tune has trapped us on the roof forever so we're probably unlikely to be popping down to serve him today.

EDDIE (*Looking down.*) No, that's not going to work.

RICHIE Why not?

EDDIE Because he's lying on the pavement unconscious with a bell in the back of the head. Oh hang on, hang on, someone's coming to help him . . . oh no, they're not, no they're just nicking his wallet.

RICHIE Have they got his wedding ring yet?

EDDIE Well, not yet.

RICHIE Well come on, let's get down there, you know what vultures they're like round here.

EDDIE Look we cannot get off the roof!

RICHIE Oh, don't be ridiculous, there must be some way. Well couldn't we make a parachute out of your trousers?

EDDIE Well, we could make an aircraft hangar out of yours.

RICHIE Don't you start calling me Mr Wobbly Bottom, young lad.

EDDIE And why not, Mr Two-Planets-Colliding in a pair of pants.

RICHIE Well you're a fine one to talk. Every time you bend over it's like watching two Zeppelins having it off.

EDDIE Look, this is no time for a discussion about the vastness of your bottom, we have got to get off the roof you madman – they're looting the shop! They are! They're looting the shop!

RICHIE What?!

Rushes to the edge.

RICHIE You put those Frosties back immediately. You bring back that Dream Topping! I'm writing all this down you know!!! I know who you are! And once I find out your names you'll all be for the high jump!!! That's it, Eddie. Jump! Why don't you jump? Go on. It's only you. You'd be doing a service – you might even get a George Cross.

EDDIE I might get two broken legs.

RICHIE The drainpipe. I'm a genius! Look, it's staring us right in the face. All right. Off you go old mate. Go on. Off you go.

EDDIE No, no. Why don't you go?

RICHIE Because I've got mayonnaise all over my face. What would they think? You bring those shelves back!! This is getting serious. This is going to cost us a fortune.

EDDIE Money?!!

RICHIE Yeah. We're going to have to pay for all of this!

EDDIE Right! I'm on my way.

Climbs over the side.

RICHIE Ooooh I forgot about the string.

EDDIE What string?

The drain pipe moves away from the wall.

RICHIE The string that holds everything onto the e . . .

Eddie and drainpipe disappear and there is a loud crash.

RICHIE Eddie! Are you all right? (*Inaudible answer.*) Is the car? That's it, now fight off all the looters . . . yeah. Get the big one with the tattoos . . . no, you're supposed to hit him . . . look forget it, just come inside and lock the doors of the shop and come up here and get me off this bloody roof!

SCENE FIVE – SHOP/ROOF

Eddie is forcing the door shut. People are trying to get in.

EDDIE And stay out.

He runs through a now looted shop to the door leading to the boys' flat.

I'm coming Richie!

Richie, meanwhile, has gathered things up.

RICHIE That's the last time I'm coming up here on this wretched roof. Why can I never remember the old maxim, 'If you want to have a good time – forget it'.

Eddie is now on the top landing and goes through the hatch. He comes up through the hatch.

EDDIE Tara!!!!

The trap door slams behind him.

Thunder and lighting. It rains on them. Richie and Eddie circle each other. Richie punches Eddie. Eddie flies off the roof.

Freeze.

Fin.

BOTTOM ACCIDENT

SCENE ONE – LIVING ROOM

We see Eddie sitting despondently at the kitchen table. Richie enters.

RICHIE Happy birthday to me,
Happy birthday to me,
Happy birthday dear Richie,
Happy birthday to me.

Pause.

Happy birthday to me,
Happy birthday dear Richie,
Happy birthday to me.

Richie looks expectantly at Eddie. Eddie gives in.

EDDIE Happy birthday Richie.

RICHIE Thank you. Rather a bumper crop of cards this year. Popular guy you see Eddie. Let's see . . . how many cards did you get for your birthday? Oh no, no of course, how thoughtless of me. 'Cause you didn't get any did you?

EDDIE Only because you glued up the letter box.

RICHIE Now that's just sour grapes Eddie, there was absolutely no proof that it was me.

EDDIE Well, except you couldn't get your hands out of your pockets all day. (*Pause.*) Mind you, what's new?

RICHIE Seventeen!!! (*Reads.*) 'May all your birthdays be happy ones, we like you more than Eddie'. Ah. That's nice isn't it? 'Terry Hardacre', ha ha ha, he's written a little joke. 'Congratulations, it's your birthday, it's time for lots of fun . . .

Eddie mouths along with Richie.

. . . so roll this card up nice and tight, and stick it up your bum.' Ha ha ha ha! He is a madman. Unstoppable!

EDDIE That's the same card he sent last year isn't it? That's the same one he's sent for the last five years actually. Same joke as well.

RICHIE Ooh, I wonder who this one could be from?

Eddie peers at it from across the table.

EDDIE That looks like the one from Sue Carpenter.

Richie opens it. Looks aghast.

RICHIE Eddie! You must be psychic. It is! It's from Sue Carpenter. Good old Sue. (*He kisses the card.*) I really must phone her up more often.

EDDIE I don't think you should Richie, they took out that injunction remember?

RICHIE Oh, here's one from 'All the lads on the Ark Royal'. Bless 'em. They never forget an old serviceman.

EDDIE By 'serviceman' I take it you mean that time you got caught on board pretending to be the captain. Just to impress Ethel Cardew.

RICHIE It worked.

EDDIE No it didn't – she got off with the arresting officer.

RICHIE Yeah. Well it worked for him. Anyway, stop trying to spoil my birthday. Look, it says here, 'Best wishes from all the lads on the Ark Royal'.

EDDIE But it's in your handwriting! You've been sending it to yourself for the last seven years. (*Without opening them.*) This one's from Rod Steiger, this one's from Abba with, 'Happy Christmas 1973' written inside it, and this one's from 'The People of the Soviet Union, in grateful thanks to Comrade Richie'.

RICHIE It's in Russian!!!

EDDIE You just put the 'r's the wrong way round.

RICHIE That's what Russian is!

EDDIE God, every year we have to go through this ridiculous charade.

RICHIE God you're weird aren't you? I mean, you're really weird. This is all because I accidentally ruined your birthday last year isn't it? Well it wasn't my fault I got so terribly ill I had to order you to cancel your birthday party.

EDDIE You weren't ill. You just ate a tin of curry powder and painted your face green. I knew it was a hoax because the paint washed off when that enema backfired.

RICHIE OK, OK, OK, let's sort this out. Now we're good friends Eddie, we've known each other for a long time. We can talk and there is something I've been meaning to say to you for the last twenty-five years.

EDDIE Oh? What's that?

RICHIE I hate you, I hate you, I hate you. Go away and crawl away in a ditch somewhere you bastard!!!!!!

Pause. Eddie looks terrified.

EDDIE It was just a joke.

RICHIE No it wasn't. Was it?

EDDIE Of course it was. I know these cards are genuine. The guys from the Ark Royal. (*Pointing to another card.*) General Pinochet, I mean how could you fake something like that? Ha ha ha. I was just joking. I'm sorry.

RICHIE Are you?

EDDIE Yes.

RICHIE Well write it down then.

EDDIE What?

RICHIE Go on, there's a pen. Write down, 'I'm sorry'. Write down, 'I'm sorry I'm a twat'. Write down, 'I'm sorry I'm a twat' ten times. I shall wait for you by the television until you're ready.

Eddie starts writing.

EDDIE 'I'm sorry I'm a twat ten times.'

He finishes and hands it to Richie.

EDDIE There you go.

RICHIE You're forgiven. *And*, you can come to my birthday party tonight.

EDDIE Your what? I was going to go out tonight.

RICHIE What?

EDDIE Yeah, I was going out with my real friends.

RICHIE Well . . . well, they can come too, so long as they bring a bottle. And don't steal all my birds.

EDDIE Well who on earth's coming to this party?

RICHIE Well I don't know. Just twenty or thirty of my closest chums.

EDDIE Who's confirmed?

RICHIE Oh Eddie, you're so old fashioned. Nobody confirms invites these days. They just sort of turn up when they feel like it. It's a very informal easy-going sort of arrangement. I very much approve. It's a breath of fresh air if you ask me.

EDDIE So no one's confirmed?

RICHIE That's right – no one. It's great.

EDDIE Mmmmmmmnn.

RICHIE Oh, by the way Eddie!

He makes a strange gesture.

E-heh-heh-heh-heh.

EDDIE What are you doing now?

Richie repeats the gesture then sings very quietly under his breath.

Happy birthday to me . . .

EDDIE Oh I see.

Fishes something out of his back pocket and hands it to Richie.

EDDIE Happy birthday Richie.

RICHIE Oh Eddie you shouldn't have. You know I don't like anyone to make a fuss of my birthday. It's a bit small isn't it? Is this how much you value our relationship? Oh well, what the hell. I may as well be nice about it.

Deep breath.

Ooh, I wonder what it is.

Opens it.

Oh it's a comb.

Pause.

It's my comb. It's my comb that I lost last week.

EDDIE And now I'm giving it back to you. Happy birthday.

RICHIE Look, this isn't some sort of joke you know – this is my birthday. Now you take this wrapping paper and you get me something good, or else.

EDDIE All right, all right.

Eddie turns and quickly picks something out and wraps it then gives it back to Richie.

EDDIE Happy birthday!

RICHIE Ooh! That's a bit more like it. That's bigger isn't it? I wonder what it is? I wonder what it is?

Shakes it. Rattles it.

RICHIE It's . . . it's . . . the remote control from the television set.

EDDIE That's right. What do you want to watch, birthday boy?

RICHIE Right that's it Eddie, this time you have really overstepped the mark. It's a fight!

Eddie shrinks back from Richie's advance. Richie swings and misses.

EDDIE Hang on, hang on, hang on, hang on. I've got your real present here.

He takes out a bit of paper and waves it.

RICHIE It's a piece of paper, it is a small piece of paper!

EDDIE Read it!

He give it to Richie. Richie reads.

RICHIE Madame Swish, three-thirty.

Looks amazed.

RICHIE Ooh Eddie you haven't? Oh what a pal you are. Madame Swish? Ooer. God, at last I'm really going to do it. And on my birthday as well. Oh, I wonder what she's like?

EDDIE She's a dead cert, mate – a real stayer.

RICHIE Really?

EDDIE Yeah, she'll come first.

RICHIE What, before me? Good grief, that's quick. So she'll think I'm great. Oh what a pal you are. And it's all paid for?

EDDIE Not exactly, I need a tenner.

RICHIE A tenner? Right that's quite cheap isn't it?

EDDIE Well no, in that case, it's a tenner each way.

RICHIE (*Gulps.*) Well how many ways are there?

EDDIE Well you'll come first, second or third, won't you?

RICHIE Well how many people are going to be there?

EDDIE Well, a few thousand.

RICHIE What?

EDDIE Well it's Kempton.

RICHIE Kempton? I can't get down to Kempton by three-thirty.

EDDIE You don't have to mate, it'll be on the telly.

RICHIE They're going to televise it? What if my Aunty's watching?

EDDIE Well what's illegal about betting on a horse?

RICHIE A horse?

EDDIE Yeah.

RICHIE Madame Swish is-is-is a horse?

EDDIE Yeah, why? What did you think it was?

RICHIE Oh no, nothing, nothing, I was just checking.

EDDIE I have given you a red hot tip.

RICHIE I know and there's nothing I can do about it now is there?

EDDIE That horse is an absolute cert, it's a fantastic birthday present.

RICHIE I'm sorry Eddie, I'm sorry. I was just being silly. Well how much shall I put on it?

EDDIE Give us twenty quid and I'll see what I can do.

RICHIE OK, there you are old mate.

Gives him £20.

EDDIE Thanks mate. Happy birthday.

He leaves.

SCENE TWO – FLAT, LIVING ROOM

Richie is on top of a ladder, putting the finishing touches to his party decorations. He is holding a fairy doll which he is about to put on the top of a Christmas tree.

RICHIE Happy birthday to me da da da,
Happy birthday,
Happy birthday to you,
Happy birthday,

He looks up the doll's skirt.

Happy birthday to me.

Eddie comes in, barging through the door and nearly knocking Richie off his ladder. He is carrying a box full of booze.

RICHIE Ooh! Careful Eddie! Well did we win?

EDDIE No, we lost.

RICHIE Damn!!!!

EDDIE Only joking.

RICHIE You mean we won?

EDDIE Yep indeedy-do.

RICHIE Fantastic! I knew I was great. What were the odds?

EDDIE Ten to one.

RICHIE Ten to one! Is that good?

EDDIE Well you gave me ten didn't you – so you get one. Ten to one.

Richie leans down and takes the pound coin and puts it in his pocket.

RICHIE Brilliant! What a fantastic birthday present. Hey, hang on, hang on a minute. I gave you two tenners.

EDDIE Ho ho ho, caught me out hey?

RICHIE Yeah, you don't get much past old Richie.

EDDIE Yeah, you're right there. Here's your other quid.

He takes a huge wedge of fivers out of his pocket to get to his spare change.

RICHIE Great! Two quid! I knew today was my lucky day. Toss it over . . . .

Eddie flicks the coin towards Richie. He turns and starts unpacking his box of booze. Richie tries to catch the other quid and falls off the ladder.

. . . ooooh!

He lands awkwardly. One of his legs is facing the wrong way. He is in absolute agony. He sees his foot.

Oh God – shit! What's that doing there? Eddie! Help! Eddie! Eddie! My leg's pointing the wrong way!

EDDIE Well point it the right way!

RICHIE Ow! Ow! I can't.

EDDIE Hang on I'll give you a hand.

Eddie grabs Richie's leg and starts trying to pull it round to the proper position. Richie screams and screams.

EDDIE Hang on, I'll try it from a different angle.

RICHIE OK.

He moves round to another position, jams his foot against Richie's face for support, and pulls with all his might. Richie screams more and more.

EDDIE It's no good, it won't budge.

RICHIE Get the ambulance.

EDDIE We haven't got an ambulance. Anyway, we don't need one. Because I've just had a fantastic idea.

Eddie starts to rig a contraption between Richie's leg and the door.

RICHIE Oh God, oh God, oh God. I'll never walk again! I'll never play tennis! You'll have to carry me to the toilet. Ur! You'll see my nob!

EDDIE Right. Now just relax because you might feel a moment's discomfort!

RICHIE Okay.

Eddie takes a run at the door and closes it as hard as he can. It's the old tooth extraction ploy. Richie's leg doesn't alter it's position in relation to Richie's body, instead his whole body is dragged skidding along the floor.

Richie's head hits the door hard, the impact knocks a plaster Father Christmas onto his head.

SCENE THREE – THE FLAT. LIVING ROOM HALLWAY/UPSTAIRS BROOM CUPBOARD

Eddie is wheeling Richie back into the flat. Richie is in a wheelchair. His leg is plastered up to the groin.

RICHIE Forwards. Stop. Stop. Stop.

Eddie crashes Richie under the table.

I'm stuck, I'm stuck.

Eddie moves to free him.

Right. I'm fine here, just leave it. I'm fine Eddie. No, that's fine, that's fine. Oh God. Thank God we're home.

Eddie pulls Richie free.

I couldn't believe that nurse! All I said was, 'Hello, have you seen *The Singing Detective*?', and she twatted me with a kidney dish! Right, what time is it?

EDDIE Five to seven.

RICHIE Right, that gives us five minutes. OK Eddie, I'm relying on you old chum – you've got to finish the decorations, put out the eats, sort out the drink, and everything will be lovely. Now, there's at least twenty people coming – so you'd better put out *both* bags of nuts.

EDDIE Okey dokey.

RICHIE Now, what about music? Better have something on for when they come in. I know, Chris Montez. If he's not sexy, I'm a ridiculous old prat.

He wheels himself over to the record player and knocks it off the table with his plastered leg.

RICHIE Oh bugger! Fix this bloody thing Eddie, why do I have to do everything round here?

Eddie comes over and fixes it.

EDDIE There you go, arsehole.

RICHIE I beg your pardon?

EDDIE I said, 'I've fixed the record player old buddie.'

RICHIE All right, all right, well there's no need to brag about it, anyone could have done it. Go on, skidaddle, you haven't even got your nuts out yet? Here we go.

He puts on the Chris Montez record, 'The more I see you'. Richie sinks into reverie. Eddie is dispersing nuts about the room.

RICHIE Oh, this is great, isn't it Eddie? Hey! Listen to this bit . . . Oh! Isn't that great? It really gets you doesn't it?

He starts moving about in his wheelchair, embarrassingly.

RICHIE Ouch, oublyia, oublyia, shake that thang! I could've been a dancer you know. They wouldn't let me into the ballet school – said I was too old.

EDDIE When was this?

RICHIE Last week.

He sinks back into the music.

Cor, isn't this great? No wonder it sends the birds crazy. That reminds me. You'd better change the sheets on my bed in case I get lucky.

EDDIE What – with the lads from the Ark Royal?

RICHIE (*Hoarse exhalation.*) Eddie you old rogue. Oh I'm in a good mood, do I look great? I tell you, by the time I'm finished there won't be a bird left alive in this place.

EDDIE (*Looking quizzical.*) How many birds did you invite then?

RICHIE None! You don't invite birds! They just turn up! Put the word about down the pub, 'Richie's having a party' – this place'll be jammed by midnight.

The record comes to a stop with a huge scratch.

RICHIE Shall I put it on again or do you want to hear something else?

EDDIE What else have you got?

RICHIE I've got the flipside!

EDDIE Ooh no more music for me thanks – I think I'll go insane with pleasure.

RICHIE Can't take the pace heh? Well I think we'll have the 'A' side again. If you can't stand the heat get out of the kitchen.

EDDIE But I'm in the living room.

RICHIE I know – it's a Spoonerism. Oh forget it – I was just being fashionable. Christ what time is it?

EDDIE It's exactly thirty seconds to seven o'clock.

RICHIE Is it? Damn I've got no time to put on my girl-bait underpants. Right, give us a countdown to the last final few seconds old mate.

EDDIE Okey dokey. Five, four, three, two, one. Zero!

Richie opens the door.

RICHIE Ha-a-a!

There is no one there.

RICHIE Right well that's it – it's a disaster isn't it?

Eddie nods.

RICHIE Right well, it's a simple equation – I haven't got any friends; so I'm going to kill myself. Eddie, go upstairs and get the razor blades.

EDDIE Right you are old mate. What do you want? Safety or non-safety?

There is a knocking at the door. Richie spins in his chair.

RICHIE Oh hurrah! They're here at last! Playing the old 'I'm late' gag to the hilt. What great mates I've got.

More knocking at the door. Richie moves to the front door in his wheelchair.

RICHIE Wait! I'm coming! I'm coming! Had an accident. I'm not very quick. Don't go. Don't go away. Here I am.

Finally gets to the door and opens it with a flourish.

RICHIE Welcome one and welcome all!

Hedgehog and Spudgun stand there uncomprehendingly. Richie falters.

RICHIE Who on earth are you?

SPUDGUN Hmmmm, sorry, we seem to have come to the wrong house.

HEDGEHOG We're looking for 'Chopper' Hitler.

RICHIE Chopper!!!??? Is there something I don't know Eddie?

EDDIE Hello boys, come on in, don't mind him, he's just waiting for his mates to turn up.

They move into the living room.

EDDIE Right here we go then. Here's the punch, get stuck in.

SPUDGUN Thanks, Eddie. My wife's gone to the West Indies.

EDDIE I didn't know that.

SPUDGUN Yeah, she went on Tuesday. (*Pause.*) It was funnier in the pub.

EDDIE You not having a drink?

HEDGEHOG Well we haven't got time have we? Not if we're going to this party?

EDDIE No, I'm afraid this is the party.

HEDGEHOG Oh.

Richie makes that coughing-to-get-attention noise. Richie wheels into the group and forces Hedgehog to put down his glass.

RICHIE Excuse me, excuse me, could you put that down please? Just put that down!

HEDGEHOG Why, what's wrong with it?

RICHIE Never mind that, can I have your names please.

EDDIE Richie, these are my friends that you said I could invite, Spudgun and Dave Hedgehog.

RICHIE Oh well, this is rather difficult for me, because you see you've only really been half-invited. You're not on the A-list. But as it is my birthday, I will let you stay. But I'm afraid I can't really let you stay properly. So I'm going to have to ask you to stand in that corner please.

un, Hedgehog and Eddie move to the corner of the large empty room.

RICHIE Quicker! Right, now that's fine. Now stay there. If you want to go to the toilet, put your hand up. I'm just going to see if anyone's come yet.

Pause. Richie wheels himself to the middle of the room. He looks at his watch and keeps looking towards the front door. Hedgehog picks up the nerve to speak.

HEDGEHOG I see they've put up a new 'Give Way' sign at the junction then.

EDDIE Yeah.

SPUDGUN Hmmmmn.

RICHIE J-j-j-j-j . . . can you just keep it down a bit please? Good grief!

Pause.

SPUDGUN They've painted the road markings to match – did you see that?

EDDIE I did, yeah.

HEDGEHOG I did too.

RICHIE For Christ's sake! Can't you keep a lid on it for a moment? I can't hear if anyone's knocking on the door or not. There could be thousands of them all queuing up on the stairs by now. Oh Christ. I suppose I'll just have to go and check. And no wandering into the middle of the room while I'm away.

Richie exits into the hall.

Spudgun puts his hand up.

SPUDGUN Do you think he'll be a long time?

EDDIE I'd do it in your glass mate.

Spudgun pees into his glass.

Richie wheels himself to the front door and opens it. No one there. We see on his face that he knows no one is coming to the party.

RICHIE Hello? . . . Is anyone coming?

(*Sighs.*) Happy birthday to me,
Happy birthday to me,
Happy birthday dear me-e-e,
Happy birthday to me.

Pause, sighs. Nearly cries. He has a thought. Madness creeps across his face. Then loudly to imaginary guests.

RICHIE I'm sorry you can't come in! It distinctly said on the invite, 'No jeans'. And you – where's your bottle? – Well you can't come in either then. And you twenty birds – I told you – no bikinis – bugger off! In fact, I've decided none of you can come in. That's right, all two thousand of you, bugger off! I've decided I'd rather play with Eddie and his friends.

Cut to Eddie and chums in the corner of the lounge. Huge sighs of disappointment.

Richie knocks on the door. Then opens it.

(*Out of view.*) Yes? Well I don't care if you are Valerie Singleton in the nude – bugger off!

In the living room, Spudgun is looking at the glass of pee.

EDDIE I think you should see a doctor, mate.

Richie comes back into the living room.

Guys, guys – I've fixed it. Come on out of the corner – I've fixed it so you don't have to stay there anymore. I don't know if you overheard me at all or not but I told everyone else to go away. Yeah, yeah I did. I thought, you know, 'Let's just have a nice little private party, me, Eddie and his two great mates' – I mean we're the hardcore aren't we? Come on, drinks all round.

Eddie and chums move out of the corner and gravitate towards the drinks table.

Spudgun puts glass of pee in front of Richie.

So mate, em tell me about this roadsign, sounds great.

SPUDGUN Is it all right to talk Eddie?

Eddie nods.

Well, they've put up this new road sign, which says, 'Give Way'. But, like, the thing is, the old one said, 'Give Way' as well, so there's no real difference, they're just the same. So what I was saying was why did they put up the new one? I mean everything would have just been the same.

RICHIE Oh! Oh! (*Huge fake laughter.*) That's incredible! We're really the guys aren't we? Hey I know. Let's all get completely drunk and play Postman's Knock. Where's that sherry?

Richie picks up the glass of pee and drinks.

RICHIE Eugh! It's a big warm isn't it?

SPUDGUN So, what's Postman's Knock then?

RICHIE Oh right, well . . . well mate . . . what's your name again?

SPUDGUN Spudgun.

RICHIE Spudgun . . . why do they call you Spudgun?

SPUDGUN Give me a potato and I'll show you why.

RICHIE Oh!

EDDIE No don't Rich – you don't want to see that.

RICHIE Well why do they call you Hedgehog?

HEDGEHOG Give me a hedgehog and I'll show you why.

EDDIE Why don't we just move on, eh? What are the rules to this fantastic Postman's Knock?

RICHIE Oh right. It's great. Right. All the birds sit round in a circle, right? Then I go out into the hall and one by one, all the birds come out and snog me.

He looks round at their worried faces.

Right, so we'll give that one a miss shall we? I know – what about Sardines?

SPUDGUN What about them?

HEDGEHOG Well they're a kind of fish aren't they?

RICHIE (*More huge fake laughter.*) That's right – they are! We're all incredible aren't we? What a great time we're having! No, but let's be sensible for a moment and sort out the rules. Right, Sardines is a game, right. One of us goes outside and hides and all the others have to come and look for him, but when they find him they hide with him. And snog with him. If they want to. Er. If they're a bird right? Which we're not. So we probably won't. I don't know – maybe give it a try. No we won't give it a try. OK? So, who wants to go and hide?

Puts his hand up.

Me!!! Ha ha, fooled you there! Right, close your eyes and off we go. Close your eyes. (*Slaps Hedgehog.*) Just stop peeking. Look, I know we're great mates but you've got to do things properly.

They all close their eyes.

RICHIE All right, OK, here goes.

Richie roams around. He can't find anywhere to hide in his wheelchair.

RICHIE Damn! No good. Em. Em.

Considers going under the table.

RICHIE No, no. Eddie! Eddie! (*Whispering.*) You've got to take me upstairs and hide me in the cupboard.

EDDIE What?

RICHIE (*Whispering.*) You've got to take me upstairs and hide me in the cupboard. I can't get upstairs by myself.

Eddie looks non-plussed. He sighs.

EDDIE I can't get you up the stairs on my own.

RICHIE Well ask your great mates to help you.

EDDIE OK. (*Prods the other two.*) Right, we've got to take him upstairs and hide him in the cupboard.

RICHIE No, no don't tell them! Don't tell them! Just tell them to keep their eyes closed. We're going somewhere secret.

EDDIE Em, right, you've got to keep your eyes closed because it's a secret that we're going to hide him in the cupboard. OK, right. Let's go.

Keeping their eyes closed, they lift Richie and the wheelchair out of the room and up the stairs.

RICHIE Keep your eyes closed. Careful, careful. Left, left here. Steady guys. Keep your eyes closed. Eddie, keep your eyes closed. Come on. Up we go. Up we go. Come on push.

This is supposed to be fun. Careful, careful. Keep your eyes closed, keep your eyes closed. Right. Put me down. Good. Right. This is going to be great. Wheel me backwards. Backwards, backwards. Isn't it nice here in the cellar. Heh heh.

Richie is in the broom cupboard.

RICHIE Right now keep your eyes closed. Run downstairs and count to ten before you start. OK?

EDDIE Right.

The three boys go back downstairs.

ALL One, two, three, four, five, six, seven, eight, nine, ten.

EDDIE Great, well that's us safe for a couple of hours. What do you fancy lads?

HEDGEHOG Let's have a drink and watch the telly.

SPUDGUN Good idea.

EDDIE Okey dokey.

He gets the drinks and switches on the TV. They all pull the chairs round and have a good watch.

EDDIE Oh great look – it's *War and Peace*! And it's only just started.

Much later. Lot's of empty beer cans everywhere.

SPUDGUN What a crap film! I knew it was going to end like that.

HEDGEHOG How do you know that?

SPUDGUN I've seen it seventeen times.

We see Richie in the broom cupboard looking at his watch.

RICHIE Four hours twenty minutes! Fabulous. That must be a new Sardines record! Wait till Norris McWhirter hears about this!

The living room.

TELEVISION ANNOUNCER And now on *Open University*, Medieval Population Distribution Patterns in Lower Saxony.

SPUDGUN What did medieval people do before telly?

HEDGEHOG Oh they probably had their tea didn't they?

EDDIE No, before telly was invented?

HEDGEHOG Ah well, they had cockfights.

Long pause.

SPUDGUN No wonder they all got the plague.

EDDIE That's Bernard Manning isn't it?

HEDGEHOG No. That's Julia Somerville.

EDDIE Oh yeah you're right.

HEDGEHOG I've done it with her.

EDDIE What? Julia Somerville?

HEDGEHOG Yeah.

SPUDGUN Done what?

HEDGEHOG Watched the news.

They are asleep. Richie is sweating in the cupboard.

RICHIE Right, that's five hours up. Got to be in the *Guinness Book of Records* by now. Where on earth is everybody? I know I'm great at Sardines but this is ridiculous.

The tv is sounding a continuous tone. Spudgun is asleep and snoring.

HEDGEHOG What – is that it then? Is that the telly done for the night?

EDDIE Hang on, I've got me *Emmerdale Farm* compilation on video if you fancy it.

HEDGEHOG Not half!

EDDIE All right I'll get the drinks in.

Later. Richie, still in the cupboard, is getting worried. He looks at this watch. Shakes it in disbelief. Opens the door a smidgen and coughs in a sort of 'I'm giving myself away' manner.

The living room. Spudgun is slumped upside down on the sofa.

EDDIE That's him, that's the one! Bastard! I hate him!

HEDGEHOG Who?

Eddie turns to look round.

EDDIE No that one there. The extra. He never says anything, he just drinks all day. Look at him! Look! He's going to buy another drink.

HEDGEHOG Is that his own money?

EDDIE No, no. They fill his pockets full of change, push him into the Woolpack and shout, 'Go on mate, drink as much as you like', and then at closing time, they give him a wage packet. Lucky bastard!

Richie – still in the cupboard. He ventures forth on to the landing. He's trying to see whether anyone's looking for him. He goes to the edge of the stairs.

RICHIE (*Sotto voce.*) I'm in the cupboard!

The living room.

RICHIE (*A bit louder.*) I'm in the cupboard!

EDDIE Oh bugger, sounds like he's rumbled our game.

RICHIE (*Off.*) Hello!

HEDGEHOG What a bastard.

EDDIE Well don't you worry, he can't get down the steps without us . . . .

RICHIE (*Off.*) Yodel-ay-dee-hoo! Aaaagh!

Richie crashes down the stairs in his wheelchair and smashes through the door at the bottom. His good leg is horribly twisted.

RICHIE Ugh! Ugh! Eddie. My other leg! Eddie!

Eddie and Hedgehog go to look at him. Both laugh.

EDDIE Hey Spudgun, come and have a look at this.

Spudgun looks, then starts to heave.

RICHIE Aaagh! (*Realises he's about to be thrown up on.*) No! No!

Spudgun throws up.

SCENE FOUR – FLAT. LIVING ROOM/FRONT DOOR/HALLWAY

A party is in full swing.

EDDIE So, he fell off the ladder and broke his leg . . . .

Everybody laughs hugely.

And then he had a bit of a motoring accident down the stairs and broke his other leg!

More insane laughter.

So I thought, well we've got all this spare booze. Why not have everyone round from the pub for a bit of a drink and a dance?

SPUDGUN Hey Eddie, do your impression again.

EDDIE All right. Pass us that mop mate. Right. Obviously be better with a lot of sweat you know. OK. 'Oh, oh, why won't anybody ever have it off with me? Maybe it's because I'm a big, fat, ugly bastard with a microscopic penis.'

Richie has just wheeled back in to witness the impression. Eddie spots him.

Hello Richie!

RICHIE What's going on here? Who are all these people?

EDDIE Em . . . these are all your friends, Richie. They turned up.

RICHIE My friends? I don't know people like this?

EDDIE Well all right, they're my friends. But it's still *your* party, no matter whose friends they are. Hey everybody! The birthday boy's here! Hurray!

Slight response.

There you are. See – look how popular you are.

RICHIE Yeah, yeah. This is my birthday party isn't it? It's a bloody brilliant one as well. Look, there must be a good, what, twelve people here. Oh all right, let's get organised.

Pulls out the lead from the record player.

Right everybody. Shut up! Shut up! I'm here at last. Hello. Right, now let's get things sorted out. I want all the boys on this side with my birthday presents and all the cracking birds on this side in a nice orderly queue ready to give me my big birthday kiss. All right. Come on, come on, look lively. You're supposed to be enjoying yourselves.

WILLY We were.

RICHIE Oh, you're the first one are you? Have you bought me a birthday present?

WILLY No.

RICHIE Ooh you'll have to have a birthday forfeit then.

WILLY What do you mean forfeit?

RICHIE This. (*Richie bops him on the nose.*) Don't mess with the party animal. Hi bird! (*He pushes her companion.*) Get out, it's not your birthday. (*To girl.*) Want to come for a ride with me? Hey I tell you what. I know it looks like it, but that's not my leg in there.

Her boyfriend raises his arm, as if to hit Richie.

RICHIE No no no no, you can't bash the birthday boy. Not on his birthday. Look at this! See that?

Richie holds up his hand and flicks the boyfriend's willy, then turns to the rest of the room.

Right everybody! Now I've decided what I'd like to do on my birthday is play birthday charades, so all you birds, come on, get your blouses off . . . (*Approaches a girl.*) You're first mate.

He tries to grope her and she fights back.

EDDIE I think we should call the ambulance now. What d'you reckon?

Richie is still fumbling with the girl's top.

GIRL Get off me!

RICHIE It's my birthday.

BORIS What do you think you're doing with my bird you git?

RICHIE I was just going to grab her . . . Who are you?

BORIS Who are you?

RICHIE Don't you know who I am?

BORIS No, well, I mean you're obviously some sort of arsehole aren't you?

RICHIE I'll tell you who I am, mate. (*Pinching his arm.*) My name is Richard Richard. I'm the birthday boy. And don't you ever forget it.

BORIS Right, you're the birthday boy are you? Well maybe we should give you the bumps.

RICHIE Well yes. I think you jolly well should.

BORIS Shall we give him the bumps?

ALL Yeah.

RICHIE Yeah . . . no!

WILLY Come on, how old are you?

RICHIE Two! No – one! Help!

EDDIE Happy birthday Richie, break a leg!

RICHIE No! No!

They give him the bumps.

Richie's legs snap and he lets out a scream.

Freeze.

Fin.

CAST LISTS

BOT

BottomSmells Tuesday 17th September 1991

Richard Richard (Richie) .... **Rik Mayall**
Edward Hitler (Eddie) .... **Adrian Edmondson**
Mr Sex .... **Kevin McNally**
Woman at bar .... **Harriet Thorpe**
Woman's Husband .... **Clive Mantle**
Landlord .... **Lee Cornes**
Kate .... **Cindy Shelley**
Jenny .... **Carla Mendonca**

BottomGas Tuesday 24th September 1991

Richie .... **Rik Mayall**
Eddie .... **Adrian Edmondson**
The Gasman .... **Mark Lambert**
Mr Rottweiler .... **Brian Glover**
Lolly .... **Gabi Valenti**

B O T

Bottom Contest Tuesday 1st October 1991

Richie .... **Rik Mayall**
Eddie .... **Adrian Edmondson**

Bottom Apocalypse Tuesday 8th October 1991

Richie .... **Rik Mayall**
Eddie .... **Adrian Edmondson**
Shooting Gallery Stallholder .... **Mark Arden**
Brenda the Ballgazer .... **Liz Smith**
Nurse .... **Helen Lederer**
Sir Roger Cobham .... **Roger Brierley**

T O M

Bottoms Up Tuesday 15th October 1991

Richie	**Rik Mayall**
Eddie	**Adrian Edmondson**
Mr Harrison	**Roger Sloman**
Mr Cooper	**Michael Redfern**
Doctor	**John Wells**
Old Lady	**Evie Garratt**

Bottom Accident Tuesday 29th October 1991

Richie	**Rik Mayall**
Eddie	**Adrian Edmondson**
Spudgun	**Steven O'Donnell**
Hedgehog	**Christopher Ryan**
Boris	**Mark Williams**
Willy	**David Lloyd**

B O T

T O M

T O M